THE SUCCESSFUL
Project Manager

Practical Guidance
from Lessons Learned

DONNA D. GREGORIO

Donna D. Gregorio is a department head and project manager at:

MITRE | SOLVING PROBLEMS FOR A SAFER WORLD

The author's affiliation with The MITRE Corporation is provided for identification purposes only and is not intended to convey or imply MITRE's concurrence with, or support for, the positions, opinions, or viewpoints expressed by the author.

Approved for Public Release; Distribution Unlimited. Public Release Case Number 21-0606.

ISBN: 979-8-7364616-0-8

Printed in the United States of America

CONTENTS

Chapter 1
INTRODUCTION

The 3 primary forces behind project management are: (1) the growing demand for complex, customized goods and services. (2) the exponential expansion of human knowledge; and (3) the global production-consumption environment.

— Project Management: The Managerial Process

How would you like it if you worked hard for six months as a project manager (PM) and then your whole team of PMs got replaced? Or if your project were to be cancelled without any notice? Or if your project were to be put on hold for a year?

As PMs, we often get wrapped up in creating schedules and developing administrative details rather than focusing on project execution. Although doing what we are told, the status-reporting PM services can become extraneous. PMs need to be irreplaceable, not irrelevant. With so much to manage, how do you know where to focus your energy? How do you know which game-changer techniques to use in each phase of complex projects to drive project success?

You want more successful projects and better techniques for course corrections. You want a guide to project management that avoids technical jargon while focusing on critical tools rather than providing a long list of options that can be difficult to sort through. You want professional success, positive results, and the confidence to take on today's innovative projects.

I'm going to show you precisely how to handle complex challenges that are typically found at each project stage until you have mastered everything necessary to get your desired results. The practical material presents complex use cases, highlights what went wrong, and discusses the game-changer techniques for helping fix potential challenges that can arise. With increasing reliance on innovation and collaboration, these tools are more important than ever.

Even your stellar execution of these project management principles may still result in an unsuccessful project. Many things can go wrong that are out of your control, such as shifts in budgets, technology, support, or timing. The worst result of your PM efforts occurs when the project fails to deliver on the outcome. It is in your best interests to master your leadership skills that are firmly under your control, and this practical guidance can provide you with the roadmap needed to manage that complexity.

I have experienced these real-life stories and have taught these game-changer techniques at the college level. While putting together my syllabus, my junior PM students appreciated and valued these stories. Rather than trying to teach all the tools, my course focused on my experiences with the critical tools that I have found effective in moving from project rescue to preventing project mishaps.

I have been a PM and business analyst (BA) for most of my over 30-year career, with professional certifications in both fields. I have applied skills as an information technology (IT) manager, and have taught project management at the graduate level. Of the over 100 projects that I have worked on, I estimate that 50% of them posed challenges, and this book is designed to annihilate the biggest challenges from your future work program.

Early career project managers and business analysts will use these techniques to be better PMs and understand the impact of their execution on successful projects. This book describes the what and why of project management, plus the how, including illustrative stories and examples to plan your next moves. Even though current PM and BA guidance is abundant, such as the standard Project Manager Institute (PMI), Project Management Body of Knowledge (PMBOK), and the International Institute of Business Analyst (IIBA), Certified Business Analyst Professional (CBAP) documents, one size does not fit all. In the complex world of IT, PM and BA roles are converging. You need to learn how those in the two professions should collaborate for maximum effectiveness.

Project management skills produce schedules, resource plans, tasks, and outcomes that are tangible, well-defined, and focused on business success. Project managers schedule meetings, check on progress, produce stakeholder reports, and guide teams to the end zone. Without their skill and prowess, many projects would not get off the ground, let alone be successful. The key competencies of a PM include leadership, communication, organization, interpersonal skills, as well as the qualities of consistency, honesty, adaptability, technical savvy, enthusiasm, and professionalism.

> *"The 3 prime objectives of project management are to meet specified performance within cost and on schedule."* (Project Management: The Managerial Process)

Management will rely on the PM to define the budget and key milestones, as well as a quality business outcome. Deriving these three key results are critical to project success. You should focus on things that are important such as relationship building, critical issues, deadline-driven products, and risk mitigation. You can make a difference by finding solutions. Do not be limited by business-as-usual.

Business analyst skills help you define requirements, build process maps, and understand workflow. You will use these skills to interview stakeholders, apply technical expertise, and question direction. They can help you understand integrations, build prototypes, and recommend alternatives. Without these skills, many projects would miss the business need and fail to achieve to a successful technical solution. The organizational skills of a project manager combined with the inquisitive technical skills of a business analyst have provided the right mix of abilities on projects throughout my career.

The knowledge areas of the Business Analyst Body of Knowledge (BABOK) are:

- Business Analysis Planning and Monitoring: organize business analysis efforts

- Elicitation and Collaboration: conduct elicitation activities and confirm the results

- Requirements Life Cycle Management: manage requirements and design

- Strategy Analysis: identify business need, and align change strategy

- Requirements Analysis and Design Definition: organize and specify requirements and designs, validate information, identify solution options, and estimate value that could be realized

- Solution Evaluation: assess performance of and value delivered by a solution and recommend improvements on increasing value

(BABOK: Business Analyst Body of Knowledge)

For me personally, the crucial BA skills have consistently been the key for strategy analysis, requirements analysis, and design definition. Repeatedly, these skills have helped me drive the business forward to mission outcome.

Combining PM and BA skills gives you more tools to apply, more credibility, and more value to make you irreplaceable. A single person not only builds the schedule but can point out weaknesses. One individual can drill down into the details and then bring things back up to a senior management level. One individual can be relied upon to know everything concerning the project, from technical details to project meetings and goals. My advice: *if you're a project manager, learn how to be a business analyst and vice versa.* These skills are not only complementary, they also combine to form solid project support.

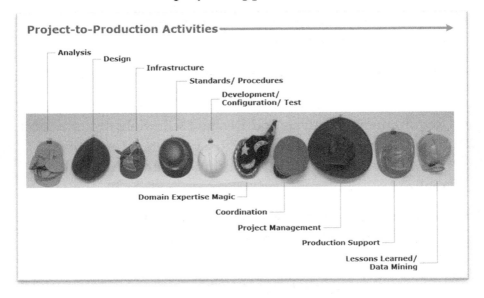

Figure 1. The Many Hats Worn by PMs (credit S. Kamener)

Figure 1 shows a photo of a colleague's office where she displayed the many hats that are worn by PMs to drive a project's success. Whether it be the skills of the inquisitive detective or the magical sorcerer, you don't have to be an expert in each of them. However, the analogy of the hats helps to explain the many roles that you need to fulfill in some capacity as we venture through project examples and case studies. The skills of both the BA and PM are represented by these hats, and that combination of technical and management talents can be the key to success in your projects and career.

A typical project has several phases, as illustrated below. Even with a waterfall or agile approach, each of these phases is addressed at least once. It could be that your project has already been approved and you have been assigned to move it along. There's no inherent need for you to read the book in order — feel free to jump from chapter to chapter to read about the part of a project that applies to your current work.

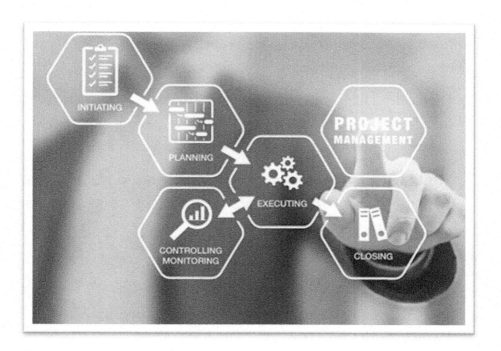

Figure 2. Project Phases

Figure 2 illustrates the classic project phases of initiating, planning, executing, and closing. In addition, monitoring and controlling are key features of the execution phase to ensure the project is on track. This book will cover each phase in a separate chapter, with summary checklists provided at the end of each one:

1. **Initiating - Laying the Groundwork:** Project kickoff, business case definition, funding, resourcing, establishing mission value and purpose

2. **Planning - Starting the Project and Breaking it Down:** Obtaining budget approval, establishing a team, identifying roles and responsibilities, stakeholders, scoping project, identifying complexity (e.g., security, privacy, Help Desk), requirements analysis

3. **Executing - Moving it Along:** Executing the project, managing tasks and interim schedules, ensuring progress, eliminating blockers, grooming the backlog, sprint execution

4. **Monitoring - What's Going On?** Reporting to stakeholders on status, probability of success, schedule progress, resource charges, budget spending

5. **Monitoring - Do We Like it?** Getting users involved, stakeholder evaluation, communication on status and progress

6. **Controlling - Does It work?** Executing test program, analysis of results, working changes back into the system, assess any showstoppers

7. **Controlling - Are We Done Yet?** Preparing to move to operational phase, stakeholder review, change readiness

8. **Closing - Wrapping It Up:** Lessons learned

Checklists are handy tools for helping project managers and business analysts to know what should be done next in project development. I always create checklists to track my To-Do List, as well as a set of repeatable items to remind me of regular reports or tasks that need to be accomplished for most projects.

In Atul Gawande's book *The Checklist Manifesto*, he says, "Faulty memory and distraction are a particular danger in what engineers call all-or-none processes: if you miss just one key thing, you might as well not have made the effort at all." This defines the need for checklists in an IT setting. Throughout the book I will provide a handy and useful checklist to summarize the best tools and techniques for reference, review, and reuse.

I am enamored with a particular online tool that enables you to create multiple sets of checklists. I have a set for my work tasks, my book clubs, my daughter's wedding planning, and even my nightly menus. My favorite checklists are the ones that help me remember to do something that I might otherwise forget. When I'm in a stressful work situation, my checklists help me get back to the basics. My arsenal of tools comes in handy when users ask for details, stakeholders ask for status, and when defining business outcomes. And to combine business with pleasure, be sure to switch over to your menu checklist to decide what to have for dinner tonight!

As I relate my reactions to what happened on some real-world projects, I will tell you about the roadblocks and challenges I have faced with real-world projects.

The first step in project management is the kickoff. This is when you set the stage for your project, define milestones, and identify yourself as a leader. Wait until you see what happens when no one wants to pay for the project.

CHECKLIST

The Successful Project Manager: Introduction

✓ Prevent becoming irrelevant by introducing game-changer techniques into your project

✓ As a PM, ensure scope, cost, and schedule are appropriate for your project

✓ As a BA, conduct planning and monitoring, elicitation and collaboration, requirements life-cycle management, strategy analysis, requirements analysis and design definition, and solution evaluation

✓ Combine PM and BA skills to help drive project success

✓ Use examples in use cases to illustrate what can go wrong and be prepared for potential challenges

Project Phases and Activities

✓ **Laying the Groundwork:** Kickoff project, establish mission value and purpose

✓ **Starting the Project and Break it Down:** Identify team, classify roles, conduct requirements analysis

---

✓ **Moving it Along:** Execute project, manage tasks, delegate work, ensure team is following the plan

✓ **What's Going On?** Report status to stakeholders, including budget and schedule

✓ **Do We Like It?** Evaluate user and stakeholder level of confidence in solution

✓ **Does it Work?** Execute test program, prioritize results

✓ **Are We done yet?** Move to operational phase, stakeholder review

✓ **Wrapping it up:** Document lessons learned, finalize budget

CHAPTER 2
INITIATING
Laying The Groundwork

Initiative pays off. It is hard to visualize a leader if she is always waiting to be told what to do. Leadership is about making others better because of your presence and making sure that impact lasts in your absence.

— Sheryl Sandberg

Ever since I was out of college, I have always wanted to own and drive a luxury car. But the sticker shock and competing expenses pivoted me to a more practical and logical vehicle purchase. Similarly, project sticker shock can result in stakeholders saying "no." Then you're left with no project, or maybe one that is less exciting, less challenging, or less critical to the desired business outcome. Make sure you know if there is enough corporate budget to cover your project's success before you launch into a vendor analysis.

This chapter discusses how the PM initiates and plans the project by creating a proposal that contains both a schedule and a budget. The pitch is often laid out in a business case or charter, in which complex outcomes and alternatives are delineated. It should include plans for any acquisitions and your team composition, especially highlighting you as the leader.

Schedules illustrate how alternatives can impact milestone dates and drive project communication, execution, and delivery. The schedule forms the basis for all work going forward and can vary in level of detail depending on the project phase. Schedules are one of the most critical PM products.

Budgets and Staff Plans should include labor, capital expenses, and any recurring costs. The most important aspect of the budget is the staff plan — managing labor delivery against planned allocation. Budgets are one of the most critical PM products.

Business cases are used to propose a project to be funded. It is a document or briefing that defines your recommended approach, options examined (e.g., journey maps), planned team, high level schedule, and budget.

Outcomes are related to the business and delineate the human impact of this effort. Products are related to the system that you are rolling out that results in that outcome. Outcomes are critical since they clarify the purpose and importance of your project.

Journey Maps are a diagramming technique that show a step-by-step view of how users execute tasks, pointing out bottlenecks and opportunities for improvement. Journey maps and similar diagramming methods are one of the most critical BA products.

Request for Proposal (RFP) is used in acquisition to purchase a vendor product. It is a contractual document that contains technical requirements, proposal instructions, and pricing format expectations.

Leadership alludes to the responsibility and ownership that PMs adopt, like convincing stakeholders that you understand each critical facet of the project and are well-prepared to take on the challenge to ensure a successful business outcome.

Characteristics that are exhibited during this phase include leadership, communication, organization, and interpersonal skills, as well as consistency, honesty, adaptability, technical savvy, enthusiasm, and professionalism.

The following case study illustrates why the planning stage needs to identify scope and cost alternatives.

CASE STUDY

Provide alternatives to avoid getting cancelled

When there were no alternative selections in cost and scope, executives had no choice but to decide against paying for a product they could not afford. Presenting a total all-in solution usually isn't enough, especially if the cost is more than is typically spent on projects. You need to be thinking ahead about these things yourself or your project will end before it begins. In a consulting organization, no one wants their project to get cancelled.

Every five years, our IT staff explores the marketplace to determine if it's worth replacing our 25-year old Human Capital Management (HCM) system. This system manages Human Resources data for 8,000 employees, including data for personnel, payroll, talent, and performance management. The As-Is application was in place for over 20 years, and our company wanted to modernize with a cloud capability that had all the latest bells and whistles.

In my role as project manager, I wrote the RFP, brought in vendors for demos, and presented a business case to recommend the purchase of a vendor product. This was an exceptionally complex task because emerging HCM commercial applications exhibit technology challenges such as cloud implementations, multiple layers of functionality, and limited customization options. Our vendor scoring sheet tracked multiple functional areas where even one area alone could be complex to implement.

Unfortunately, we had over 900 requirements, which was way too many! That meant we had to read and score each of the 900 requirements for all six vendors. And our schedule had us getting that done in two weeks, to boot!

We also had to decide how to score the inputs to agree on a quantifiable recommendation. One group wanted to score using numbers and averages to make a decision. A different group wanted to score using words (e.g., meets, exceeds requirement). I voiced my concerns that this would take far too long, and that we didn't have time to evaluate such complexity appropriately. In the end, we agreed to average the word scores manually to move the process along, but it was not without its own difficulties.

We scheduled the vendors to come on-site for all-too-familiar tool demonstrations. This resulted in a comedy of errors that may have been omens of more issues to come. One vendor flew their team to one of our sites, BUT in the wrong state (not a joke!). Another vendor team showed up and had customized their product with the wrong corporate logo. Yet another vendor team showed up to the demo an hour late, then had trouble setting up their technology, and spent the next hour apologizing for being late.

We had over 20 internal people at each vendor demo, and each demo lasted an entire day (yes, you can see the internal costs piling up quickly).

We prepared an extensive business case, such as alternatives examined (six vendors), cost assessments, benefits gained, and differences among the top two vendors. We summarized scoring charts, and described different implementation schedules. I presented the business case to stakeholders, recommending our unanimously agreed-upon vendor choice, contrasting that with the even-more-expensive runner-up vendor choice.

Our executives agreed with our plan, but no one had the budget to pay for the surprisingly expensive new system, so the project was cancelled. They agreed that it was not a matter of IF we would do this project, but it was a matter of WHEN.

There was another competing project that had a similar large price tag, and there was only enough money available for the other high priority project. Rather than assume that someone would pay, we should have prepared alternative choices. We had to take responsibility for this omission, even though they still may have chosen to fund the other competing project anyway.

When the project was cancelled, we all were disappointed — the internal team as well as the vendors. As so often happens, it's hard not to take something like this personally. Was there something I should have predicted that might have changed the outcome? However, this was purely a business decision and taking these types of decisions personally is both inappropriate and detrimental.

As difficult as it was, however, I decided to continue working on related efforts. The many work-life balance benefits provided by the company were enough to convince me that this was the best option. These consisted of social connections, my company bandmates, and the many caricatures I had collected at the company holiday parties.

Interestingly, we got the message to take another look at this project just a few years later, when our stakeholders decided they were ready to foot the bill. To complicate matters further during this time, there were executive leadership changes, including three new CHROs, a new CIO and a new COO. We used a more refined set of differentiated use cases rather than 900 requirements. We were better prepared, and we were also ready to execute a positive outcome. And guess what? After a new RFP selection effort, we picked the same vendor and product that we had chosen earlier.

Instead of presenting two vendor choices with their all-in costs, we should have worked on alternatives within the primary vendor's product offerings for cost and scope to help in the decision-making process. Rather than going all in, we might have negotiated a partial approach that would have led into the full capability over time.

There are many ways to present scope alternatives, but journey maps can visually depict alternatives from a user's standpoint. Other choices include using a spreadsheet or bullets on a slide or document. Journey maps are recommended to put decision-makers in the shoes of the user.

My recommendation is to build journey maps to show the user's perspective for both cost and scope alternatives.

The project's mission outcome was to improve employee experiences with payroll (better self-service features), benefits (enhanced elective options), and performance management (improved mechanism for the annual review process). We were stopped at the acquisition process and were not allowed to proceed until we received the green light several years later.

What is the value proposition for the business? In our case study, the successful outcome was not achieved. However, the outcome would not have been to purchase and roll out a new product. A business outcome might have included better insight into hiring or simpler access to learning modules, that would, in turn, lead to happier employees.

Journey maps can provide a detailed process flow from the user's standpoint while highlighting opportunities and bottlenecks. By presenting a set of these diagrams, stakeholders can analyze your As-Is, To-Be, and Alternative views so that they are clear on all choices. Figure 3 shows a sample journey map.

Payroll Administrator: *As-Is Journey Map*

Processing timely and accurate payroll.

	Daily Duties	Other Requests	Running payroll
Actions	• Run audit reports • Enter new hire payroll forms • Complete termination forms	• Resolve invalid codes • Pull data from HR awards • Field employee questions	• Resolve timecard issues • Update absence code balances • Prepare day-after bank documents
Bottlenecks	➤Employees to submit tax forms	➤Send files to insurance	➤Employees to resolve timecard errors ➤Send payroll file to bank
Opportunities	○Add tax change when working outside of home state	○Simplify absence codes ○Enhance self-service	○ Prevent employees from entering invalid project codes

Figure 3. Sample Journey Map

Had we created As-Is journey maps, our first step might have been to choose a user type — in this case the payroll administrator. To understand their journey, we might divide the work into workstreams such as daily duties, other requests, and running payroll. For each segment, we would interview the payroll administrators who can define specific actions in detail, identifying bottlenecks and opportunities for improvement.

Had we developed the To Be journey map, it might have shown the changes to the payroll administrator's duties with the implementation of the new system. This would have highlighted the removed bottlenecks or opportunities through the eyes of the payroll administrator and that human element.

The alternative journey maps can provide a reduced scope/cost option to the ideal payroll system. For example, imagine that you had less money to spend and wanted a less-capable version — one that enhances your payroll but doesn't automate the process, or one that does the bare minimum and sends the tax portion to an outside vendor. We could have provided those details in an alternate journey map.

In this way, the decision-makers could have seen three different journey maps: an As-Is system, a To-Be system, and an alternative To-Be system. Rather than just talk about a reduced-price option, this approach demonstrates which new features will be part of your alternative solution.

Journey maps are one of 23 curated tools maintained by our company's Innovation Toolkit Team. The team recommends and applies these tools to help PMs, clients, and collaborators to jumpstart the innovation process. Anyone with experience in facing an important challenge or project understands that the job is easier when you have the right tools. The Innovation Toolkit is a collection of methods and techniques to assist you and your team in being more innovative. Frequently-used tools in their arsenal include "persona definitions" and "premortem exercises." We refer to these tools to help analyze problem definition, complex challenges, and end-user analysis.

In general, journey maps are a great tool for viewing the system from the user's standpoint. When we re-did the RFP three years later, we used the Journey Map approach to provide differentiators to the vendors, those that would make a buy vs. not-buy decision that were deal-breakers for our specific implementation. The vendors focused their demos on each of these journeys.

Another key consideration when evaluating vendors and crucial project initiation is developing schedules. As one of the most important planning tools, we had several schedules, one for each vendor, and they played a critical role in decision-making.

Early PM work defines a business case to identify schedule, among other project-related scope items. There are many tools and techniques for building a schedule with varying degrees of ability to map dependencies, resources, and task percent complete. Suffice it to say that you need a schedule, and perhaps even a *set* of schedules to show your high-level view, your key milestones, a week-by-week view, and a detailed structure that maps dependencies and resource utilization.

All schedules start with a begin and end date and need checkpoints along the way to track progress. Milestones usually occur after a particular project phase is completed, such as testing. Time-block the schedule into date-limited stages to include interim goals and status checks. Once you have your overall project milestones in place, it is time to add tasks. Figure 4 shows a sample set of high-level schedules, including both waterfall and agile approaches.

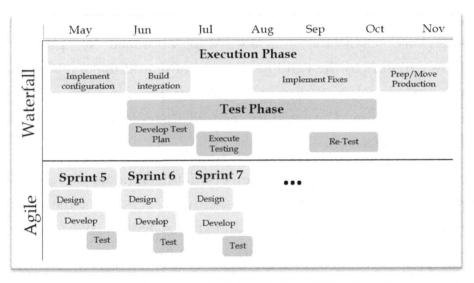

Figure 4. Sample Schedules – Waterfall and Agile

The waterfall methodology for schedule-building steps through each project phase incrementally, making sure that all requirements and design are finalized prior to implementation. The agile methodology is a more iterative approach that uses a bicycle wheel analogy, learning and implementing continually, resulting in shorter milestones and partial deliverables for stakeholder review. Both approaches have their place in project management, and you need to be familiar with both approaches. Benefits of waterfall include that it is well understood, requirements are documented, and milestones can be easily identified. Benefits of agile include that it encourages more communication, expects shorter milestones, and enables evaluation of partial results sooner.

One of the first tasks on any project schedule is to review prior lessons learned to elicit any risks from earlier similar activities. You can then drop recommended mitigation strategies into your schedule to minimize repeating prior learned mistakes. Add any key stakeholder reviews or assistance needed by related experts. Other tasks consist of relating to any old systems that are tied to this project that are being retired.

Consider phasing your project such that there are follow-on activities in place (e.g., phase 1 and 2). This way, you can add functionality over time and continue to enrich your project with added features. This approach is also beneficial if you lose funding part way through since you can better demonstrate partial progress with completion of an early phase.

In addition, tying several projects together into a larger roadmap can show how the output of one project may be used as an input for another project. This will help identify any conflicts and dependencies among other related work, such as a project portfolio.

There are many project management tools on the market that

include scheduling, tasking, budgeting, and reporting. I have used many of these tools, although certainly not all of them. My experience with automated scheduling tools is that they are required for large projects, especially if there are dependencies. I find that these tools require a lot of time to set up and maintain. Although they are time-consuming, they are very helpful and will save you time in the long run.

Typically, budget planning goes hand in hand with schedule development since the project length is directly proportional to costs and staff size. Budget planning is critical to managing complexity as one of the three legs of the stool: schedule, cost, and performance, with quality sometimes being considered as a 4th leg of the stool. Budget planning is one of the most important PM tasks.

Start defining your budget by calculating your entire level of effort for the work and itemize other needs such as subcontractors, travel, and training costs. Review your cost proposal with stakeholders to coordinate review and approval. In our case study, we neglected to do this important step prior to conducting vendor assessments.

The mechanics of budget planning require a significant staff-planning and tracking methodology. Start by assessing needed skills and identifying appropriate individuals. Create a monthly plan by person, estimating the time you anticipate will be needed to complete each task. This will be your staffing budget allocation. As time passes, you can track your actual delivery based on charges incurred to provide a regular status check of your budget delivery against actuals. Be sure to indicate your over/under charges and make staff adjustments through the life of the project to allot for cost shifts, as needed. Figure 5 shows an example of a budget that converts monthly staff estimates or FTE (full-time equivalent) into dollars using an hourly labor rate.

Staff	1-Jan	1-Feb	1-Mar	1-Apr	Total FTE	Total $
Venkat Patel	2.10	1.60	1.70	1.70	7.10	$ 1,002.65
John Smith	2.70	2.00	2.30	2.30	9.30	$ 1,313.33
Subtotal	4.80	3.60	4.00	4.00	16.40	$ 2,315.99

Figure 5. Sample Budget

Meeting project delivery means that you have succeeded to meet cost, schedule, and performance requirements. Each of these three legs of the stool are critical to your success as a project manager. Tricks to maintaining budget include managing scope and defining a clear work breakdown structure within which to manage costs and functionality. All of this adds up to PM responsibilities that continue to grow, even in the planning stage!

Being a leader of schedule, budget, and performance is not easy, and it is your responsibility to be aggressive, take charge, and pull project plans together. Leading means not just taking a seat at the table, but also demonstrating vision and making an impact so that you become irreplaceable. Waiting for others to give you direction or to do your job is ineffective. You are in charge, so confidently demonstrate that you are the right one to be the leader.

Establish yourself early in the project as a trusted advisor — the one to go to for answers, the one to solve problems and provide solutions. As a trusted advisor, you must demonstrate faith that people will work hard and be dedicated to the team and its mission. Identifying and working with stakeholders is another crucial trusted advisor role, in reporting on status and highlighting any issues.

PM leadership means establishing the cadence for regular meetings, which might be comprised of weekly meetings focused around specific executable task areas. These meetings keep people accountable, by checking on what they completed, what they are working on next, and whether there are any blockers to progress. Other project setup activities can include establishing a shared document repository, chat channels, regularly touching base with stakeholders, and budget methodology for tracking allocation against actuals.

As the PM, I pride myself in being the face of the project, and if anyone has questions, they know they can come to me. I find it necessary to strike a delicate balance between keeping stakeholders informed and keeping the team engaged through demonstrating focus, decision-making, innovation, and driving the project forward.

Summary

One of the most important kickoff tasks is schedule and budget alignment, so you need to find ways to offer alternatives in case your initial proposal is out-of-range. Alternatives in the form of journey maps can help leadership understand what they would be gaining or losing with various alternatives. The PM is critical to project kickoff, including establishing the trusted advisor relationship, creating a business case, and identifying budgets. Schedules are a critical part of project setup because they communicate, execute, and deliver on complexity throughout the lifecycle.

Alternatives help in many situations, especially when you have lost your guidance and need to come up with a way forward. PMs should not always rely on others for project direction. Frequently, there is a tangible idea dangled with a portion of the budget set aside to examine certain technology areas. However, as the PM, it is your job to define, guide, and direct a team, and that is not always as easy as it sounds. Let's now take a look at how good PM techniques can establish logical steps in the absence of clear direction.

CHECKLIST

Initiating – Laying the Groundwork

Laying the Groundwork: Kickoff project, establish mission value and purpose

✓ Define project purpose, benefits, key milestones, risks

✓ Identify alternatives and rationale for the chosen approach

✓ Convince stakeholders that project has value through clear problem definition

---

✓ Communicate with stakeholders on status and keep them abreast of any issues

✓ Clarify solution viability, feasibility, and desirability

✓ Establish your leadership by being a trusted advisor, demonstrate purpose, make an impact

✓ Focus on the three-legged stool: cost, schedule, and performance (and sometimes quality)

Tools and techniques

✓ Write business case including examined alternatives, recommended approach, cost, To-Be vs. As-Is cost analysis, risks, business outcomes

✓ Create schedule to highlight key milestones at high-level

✓ Generate budget to identify cost estimates including labor and others, such as contractors, software, etc.

✓ Identify alternative choices to evaluate all options, as well as reduced price and scope

✓ Use journey maps as a diagramming technique to show a detailed process flow from the user's perspective

✓ Document requirements in a request for proposal (RFP) if needed to buy a product

✓ Evaluate project management tools to assist in building plans for schedule, budget, and resources

✓ Define business outcomes by answering questions such as what is the value proposition to the business? How will the business succeed and be more productive?

Soft skills: Demonstrate skills of leadership, communication, organization, interpersonal, as well as the qualities of consistency, honesty, adaptability, technical savvy, enthusiasm, and professionalism

CHAPTER 3
PLANNING
Starting and Breaking Down the Project

A great team doesn't mean that they had the smartest people. What made those teams great is that everyone trusted one another. It can be a powerful thing when that magic dynamic exists.

— The Phoenix Project

When we built the house that I live in, we had plumbers and electricians ready to execute their plans. But when the general contractor became unavailable, with no guidance, the plumbers and electricians were uncertain about what work to prioritize.

What's next? That's a question your team will ask when they don't have a clear plan or direction. You shouldn't need continual direction from leadership, so you need tools and techniques to help establish deliverables and next steps.

This chapter will discuss how the PM starts the project and breaks it down into smaller executable tasks with a work breakdown structure. A project charter authorizes the existence

31

of the project and provides a reference for future direction and sense of purpose.

Work breakdown structure is a diagram used to divide the project into small, executable pieces. This forms the basis for planning, task assignments, task leadership, and schedules. This is one of the most critical tools that a PM needs to execute. You can start getting excited when your plan starts to take shape – and you own it! !

Project Charter is a document containing a detailed plan, including objectives, purpose, scope, assumptions, key outcomes, milestones, governance, and team composition.

Problem statement is a succinct definition of what your project is, why it is important, what is the eventual goal or demonstrated value, and how you plan to build it.

Use Cases are a set of actions or steps defining the interactions between a person and a system that results in a completed task. For example, as a user I want to staff my project so that I can build my team with the right skills.

Team building is a set of techniques that move your team from a group of strangers to a functioning group dedicated to helping each other yield a successful project.

Characteristics exhibited during this phase include confidence, patience, willpower, creativity, loyalty, dedication, honesty, and respect for all team members

In order to accomplish your project deliverables, you need to begin with the end in mind. This will help in meeting your schedule, avoiding delay and getting off-track. This use case will illustrate why having well-defined next steps and an end state are so important.

CASE STUDY

Keep defining next steps to avoid demonstrating slow progress

Projects can demonstrate slow progress for a variety of reasons, such as lack of guidance to poorly defined next steps. Having tools and techniques that can get back to basics can help the team brainstorm problem-solving techniques and build a path forward. No one wants to feel stuck in their project. Team members want to have tasks delegated to them so that they feel productive. But how do you move forward with limited direction?

This project was an architecture endeavor intended to address cross-functional data-sharing to solve complex challenges. It had all the right buzz words: *visibility, impact, critical,* and *long overdue.* We wrote a project charter and had lofty goals like *discover, analyze,* and *optimize.* These goals sounded more academic and less tactical. What we were missing were deliverables and outcomes. The team's first major activity was to document a minimally viable As-Is data architecture to expose the complexity of our current state, but the next steps were unclear. The project was criticized for demonstrating slow progress.

In my role as PM/BA, I defined a project charter and high-level schedule. This project was complex because of the need to manually catalog millions of data holdings, including security issues and structured vs. unstructured data.

Risks included the very real possibility that this work would turn into "shelf-ware" and not be used at all. Buy-in from leadership was not enough; we needed to convince our users that focusing on data and integrations would accelerate their project development. But how?

The first time I presented on the status of this project, after working on it for 2 months, I read from notes, afraid someone would ask me a question. I hadn't really quite figured out the project goal and felt like an imposter — not sure myself of what we were trying to do. I felt that my presentation sounded academic and was lacking in real outcomes.

Luckily, I did not get any questions, but it was one of the few times in my career when I was at a total loss, and I experienced "imposter syndrome."

As fall turned into winter, my business analyst skills had to kick into high gear. I needed to define tactical tasks and assign resources to develop deliverables. Time was quickly passing and so I kept forging ahead.

Eventually, we had to determine from the user's standpoint how this project would change the way they worked. What is the current landscape and what new capabilities are we adding? I spent countless hours with my technical team, creating slides on topic after topic, and trying out different approaches and ideas.

The key turn-around point finally came once we defined a work breakdown structure (more details on this later in the chapter). It consisted of five outcomes, each with its own set of deliverables and schedule. It helped us to communicate the five different, but related components and helped to define the tasks required in each of these categories to achieve that goal. By the time we settled on deliverables, we had collected 200 use cases, 500 business outcomes, and 95 data elements.

When someone said, the word "catalog," I thought — *bingo, that is what we are doing, lots of catalogs.* We developed briefings and lots of slides, and at one point we had a greatest hit slide deck containing all of our favorites!

Our team worked across the work breakdown structure, but they also tended to focus on their areas of strength and made significant contributions in key areas. Having short-term deliverable dates helped to keep them motivated.

As winter turned into spring, my stakeholders asked me to present a status briefing. Even though it had been months since we had provided updates, it was expected that our continued efforts were yielding results. Thankfully, I had a strong story to tell about the detailed draft deliverables, resource assignments, and a process description that made sense.

This time when I briefed, I needed no notes. I was the expert in the room, determined to answer any questions, because we had a plan, a schedule, an approach, and defined business outcomes. Our stakeholders were pleased with our results, and our project was considered a success, being rewarded with continued funding.

This project could have easily failed had we not applied those inquisitive business analyst skills to ask the hard questions and focus on tangible deliverables that would drive us to business outcomes.

As the project manager, I defined a high-level schedule and determined strategic goals, but early on we lacked anything that was actionable. Stakeholders always want to see progress on work moving forward, yet that path is not always clear, especially when the project definition is only theoretical. The project suffered from limited contact with the visionaries, so we had to define business outcomes.

When in doubt, drill down into the problem definition to create a tactical plan using a work breakdown structure. Other options for deriving problem statements include other diagramming techniques such as a mind maps, workflows, process flows, or journey maps. I have used all these approaches on a variety of projects to get at the real solution and develop the steps needed to get there.

You need to do a work breakdown structure to refine the complexity into workable pieces.

The project's mission outcome was to accelerate IT product development by enhancing the ability to find and access enterprise data more quickly. This mission was achieved, though much of the year was spent on academic exercises to decide how to do this and how to apply the analysis to our current data systems.

The Work Breakdown Structure (WBS) is my favorite tool for diving into a project and separating the deliverables into well-defined pieces that are actionable. It is one of the most important project artifacts. The WBS starts with the highest-level goals and breaks it down into a hierarchy of deliverables and outcomes one level at a time, until each manageable piece makes sense. Figure 6 shows an example of a work breakdown structure.

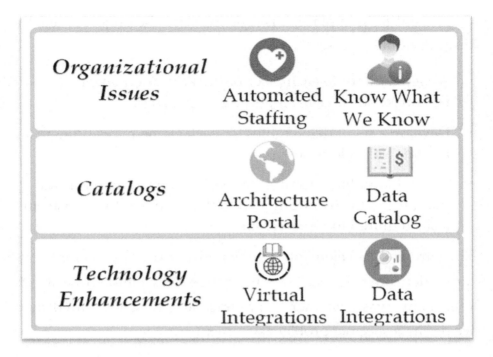

Figure 6. Sample Work Breakdown Structure

Eric Lawson defines WBS this way: "A deliverable-oriented hierarchical decomposition of the work to be executed to accomplish objectives and create the required deliverables. It organizes and defines the total scope of the project." (*Project Management — The Managerial Process 6th edition*)

Here are the types of questions you can ask to breakdown your project:

- What part will users interact with vs. other user types?

- Is there a different technology aspect (e.g., mobile or cloud)?

- Is there a part that will require a governing body to execute?

Once the WBS is in place, it is time to set up the project based on the individual pieces.

- Assign a leader to each piece of the WBS and make that person responsible for reporting on progress.

- Develop a set of deliverables for each element, resulting in a roadmap of milestones.

- Set up individual meetings for each element and refine the guest list to the team assigned to that element, to brainstorm tasks required to be successful.

The various WBS elements can be addressed in parallel if there are no dependencies between the groups. For example, one of our WBS items was customer communication, which required that we define a succinct problem statement.

The problem statement helps users understand how your project will change the way they work. The problem statement answers the following questions: What is it? Why are you building it? What is the eventual goal and demonstrated value? Why is it important? And how do you plan to get there? Figure 7 shows an example of a problem statement that answers these questions.

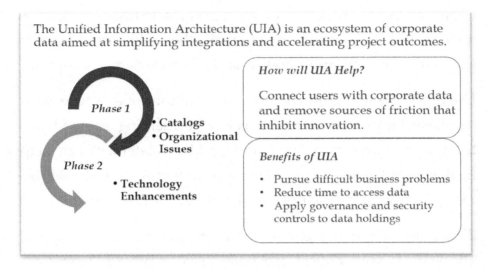

The Unified Information Architecture (UIA) is an ecosystem of corporate data aimed at simplifying integrations and accelerating project outcomes.

Phase 1

• Catalogs
• Organizational Issues

Phase 2

• Technology Enhancements

How will UIA Help?

Connect users with corporate data and remove sources of friction that inhibit innovation.

Benefits of UIA

• Pursue difficult business problems
• Reduce time to access data
• Apply governance and security controls to data holdings

Figure 7. Sample Problem Statement

Other questions that your problem statement should answer include the standard Who, What, When, Where, Why, and How questions. Who is affected by this problem? When and where does it occur? What is the value to the organization in terms of outcomes? Who else has this problem and how have they solved it already? If they have not solved it already, why not?

Write your problem statement with the audience in mind. It should not indicate or define a solution, although it may provide an idea concerning what work might complete the solution. The problem statement helps focus your goals, since if it is not specific enough, you may be trying to "boil the ocean" and never finish anything!

Your problem statement needs to cut through the jargon and be short and to the point. If your stakeholders are anything like mine, everyone is busy, so you need to speak to their needs, keep it short, and clarify how you will make their jobs easier. Discuss issues of relevance, applicability, and other barriers to adoption.

Use cases and user stories capture descriptions of a feature, with emphasis on the end user perspective. Presenting a set of high-level user stories along with the problem statement can help further detail what you are trying to accomplish. Detailed use cases are typically developed as the project progresses.

Be sure to include the team in the problem description exercise. The team is your critical backbone to your project. Teams are successful when they have good direction, connection, alignment, and performance. Forming a team takes encouragement, clarity, and guidance.

Identifying team members requires analysis of skills, availability, and other factors — including domain expertise and clearances. Minimizing turnover on a highly skilled and difficult-to-replace team includes taking care of people and paying attention to job satisfaction. Ensure the team is challenged, working skills that align with their talents, and make sure they are doing what you need them to do. Clarify everyone's expected contribution by establishing distinct roles and responsibilities.

Forming a team can take time, considering that the lineup is comprised of a collection of employees who need to mature into a unified group. D. Egnoli's *Forming, Storming, Norming, and Performing* model describes these team evolution stages.

During forming phase, team members tend to be gracious, nervous, and anticipate a great work experience, but they are unsure of their role, unclear on the mission, and trying to figure out how they will fit in. In the storming phase, people will often start to feel threatened by their peers and may reach for more authority once they determine their role. In the norming phase, the team will generally recognize their need to work together to be successful and will be more willing to ask each other for assistance. In the performing stage, the team finally gels, knows what is expected of them, and wants to see the project succeed.

I have witnessed each of these phases, to varying degrees, and although frustrating, it seems to hold true for every team on which I have been a member or leader. The longest lasting phase tends to be the forming phase when the team members are unclear of their individual roles and look to the PM for assignment. Also, since the forming phase is the least productive stage, try your best to end that stage more quickly so that you can move on to the performing stage faster, where the best work is being done.

In my experience, teams and individuals are driven by near-term deadlines. Who wants to work towards a goal that isn't expected to be done for six months? The team needs to demonstrate progress to stakeholders. Action items, reminder emails, status meetings, and regular budget updates are tools you can use to nudge your team toward achieving success. Do not mandate fake deadlines, and do not accelerate them unnecessarily as this can create way too much stress. Realistic, achievable, and actionable goals are what make teams thrive. When there is loyalty, dedication, and respect for all team members, that advances the project as well.

The final measure of a team's success is their ability to deliver a quality project on schedule and within budget. As a leader, assign work to the people with the right skills, or be willing to grow skills on the team as needed by pairing people up or sending them to training courses. Manage poor performers with honesty, check in on them more regularly, and assign more rigorous deadlines to assure that they know what is expected of them. Managing the team does not mean that you're micro-managing individuals. In my view, that is the worst way to run a team. Trust that they will deliver and check in with you as needed.

Summary

The PM needs to continually guide the team, driving the mission outcome forward, and be thoroughly knowledgeable about the project's vision, mission, and expected outcome. A tool that can help in guiding the team involves clearly defining the outcome in the Problem Statement. The Work Breakdown Structure can divide the project into executable goals and is a critical PM deliverable.

Stakeholder involvement focuses the project goals and provides a litmus test for continued progress. As the PM, it is your job to guide the narrative and push back whenever stakeholders seem inconsistent with a project's goals. Sometimes, your stakeholders give you too much to do and that can lead to "scope creep" and comes out of nowhere!

CHECKLIST

Planning – Starting the Project and Breaking it Down

Breaking it Down: Form team, classify roles, gather project requirements

✓ Define a problem statement that answer the following questions: What is it? Why are you building it? What is the eventual goal? Why is it important? And how do you plan to get there?

✓ Setup project infrastructure including a document repository, email lists, chat area

✓ Establish meeting cadence, template for regular stakeholder communication

✓ Build team that will exhibit characteristics of forming, storming, norming, and performing

✓ Assign goals to teams that are realistic, achievable, actionable, with near-term deadlines

Tools and techniques

✓ Write a project charter that identifies scope, risks, milestones, team composition, stakeholders

✓ Schedule and budget: Continue to refine and add more detail. For example, break the project into phases or provide a two-week rolling schedule to stay on top of planning

✓ Create a resource plan that includes people against time against tasking, calculate labor costs

✓ Derive a Work Breakdown Structure to dissect the project into actionable workstreams upon which to base your schedule, tasking, and outcomes

✓ Document As-Is and To-Be systems, focusing on parts that will change

✓ Elicit requirements, use cases, or user stories, as needed, and maintain this list throughout the project, such as user story backlog grooming

✓ Define data needs and document with a data dictionary, including integrations with other systems

✓ Design user interface and business processes using prototypes or flow diagrams

Soft skills: Demonstrate confidence, patience, willpower, creativity, loyalty, dedication, honesty, and respect for all team members

CHAPTER 4
EXECUTING
Moving it Along

At its root, Agile is based on a simple idea: whenever you start a project, why not regularly check in, see if what you're doing is heading in the right direction, and if it's actually what people want?

— Atul Gawande

When planning my vacation, there is a point at which I stop adding excursions and reservations in order to contain costs and just book the trip. How would you feel about a never-ending list of work that keeps growing, with new features being added to your scope regularly? This additional tasking can result in delayed schedules and incomplete projects.

As the project gets underway and requirements and user stories are put into place, this list can continue to grow beyond your original scope. Unless you are fastidious about managing the backlog of work, your project will lose sight of the critical path to success and waste time with nice-to-have features.

This chapter will discuss how the PM executes the project using either a waterfall or agile development approach. By defining an Organizational Change Management Plan to solidify the business impact, scope creep can be minimized. The PM manages a diverse and inclusive team by using Kanban boards to track task progress.

Waterfall Development approach is a linear method where all requirements are defined up front. As the system is developed, the team follows the original implementation plan, even if new things are learned.

Agile Development approach is a cyclical method where requirements are defined throughout the project in the form of user stories. Through small sprints of two to four weeks, teams incrementally build out the project and regularly demonstrate progress. Repeating the cycle continually adds user stories, as new things are learned.

Organizational Change Management Plan is a document describing how the organization's current work will change once a new system is put in place.

Scope Creep occurs when projects continually add functionality even after you have scheduled and budgeted the work. These can be wild perturbations or many small adjustments that can add up to delays and budget overruns. This is a critical PM element to manage cost and schedule.

Kanban Board is a board with columns labeled *To Do*, *In Process* and *Done*. Tasks are indicated on cards that move within the board to track progress.

Diverse and Inclusive Teams are created when individuals have different approaches to your project, based on their background, culture, and experience. For example, bringing agile methodologies into a team that is accustomed to the waterfall development approach can lead to diversity of thinking.

Characteristics exhibited during this phase include decision-making by forcing issue resolution, exercising grace and respect, providing encouragement and assistance, and second-guessing rationales for decisions to ensure they are the right ones

To define a clear end state, the PM needs to create an organizational change management plan, which will prepare stakeholders for the upcoming changes. This use case will illustrate why beginning with the end in mind can be so critical.

CASE STUDY

Maintain critical path to end state to avoid scope creep

Scope creep is a common project challenge when requirements continue to be added to the original plans. Defining a detailed end state helps minimize scope creep, which can negatively impact your project by causing schedule and budget overruns.

My company has an internal internet or *intranet* that serves as the home page for corporate news and provides links to many internal websites. When it was time to replace it with more modern technology, we expected to get a better user interface and more functionality. Our software development approach used the agile methodology, including three-week sprints, retrospectives, and user stories. Having a list of user stories meant the list continued to grow, leading to scope creep.

In my role as Scrum Master and BA, I managed the prioritized list of user stories and task list. There were no requirements defined up front, only an overall vision and major milestones.

This project was complex because of new technology, which provided limitless possibilities to create gadgets to add new functionality. We implemented customizable gadgets for corporate phonebooks, travel plans, news pages, financial status, task lists, and other sophisticated features. We even created a Phonebook Roulette gadget that showed a randomly changing employee photo, intended for employees to recognize each other. We had weather gadgets, traffic gadgets, and international clock gadgets! The more ideas we had, the more we put on the ever-growing list.

We had an agile evangelist in the department who convinced stakeholders that we should move from waterfall to agile software development. We went to training, defined user stories, and conducted daily stand-up meetings. At these meetings, we reviewed Kanban boards, which contain user stories for the three-week sprint, moved them from *To Do* to *In Progress* to *In Test* to *Done*. During the stand-up, we picked user stories to work on, and talked about what we did yesterday, what we're doing today, and what issues are preventing progress. After each sprint, we conducted retrospectives and gave demos of partially working code to critique and anticipate next steps. Most of the team was working on an agile project for the first time, and there definitely was confusion and angst over this new methodology.

We experienced that a key benefit of agile is the added level of communication through daily meetings, regular sprint review meetings and retrospectives. Another positive side effect was having interim milestones to achieve in short increments, which was a team motivator.

Each sprint produced informal deliverables, whether that was related to the software development or other related materials, such as training plans, these short-term milestones enabled additional stakeholder engagement. Some projects have limited sponsor access or sponsors are reluctant to communicate all of their needs or their needs change over time. All these issues can be assisted by the use of an agile approach where you iterate on solutions.

Our agile team consisted of a set of diverse thinkers, each with a different way of working, which led them to be uncomfortable in the strange new agile environment. Their valid concerns included things like "everyone thinks differently," "I am in the minority in my thinking and in my habits," and "I do not have the right skills for this job." They lacked confidence, suffered from being uncomfortable in a strange new environment, and second-guessed their own work. As a result, they tended not to reach out appropriately. This set of thoughts leads to a team of diverse thinkers who challenged the status quo, questioned why agile was better, and resulted in a stronger team outcome.

Having a stakeholder group would have helped manage scope creep as they could prioritize the user stories. Stakeholder negotiation may add new features while potentially removing lower priority items to balance schedule and cost. However, we did not establish such a group. We were left to our own knowledge to prioritize, which is not always easy to do. We had too many gadgets, too much excitement around the new technology, and too much flexibility.

Had we prepared an organizational change management plan, we might have introduced the changes to the employees earlier and set the stage for the critical path to success, rather than keep adding nice-to-have features.

THE SUCCESSFUL PROJECT MANAGER

Our project did finalize a conclusion and replaced the old intranet with the new version to great success. However, along the way we had our share of issues with wrapping things up. In the end, our project successes were highlighted at our final sprint review meeting by our Product Owner who had us meditate (?) on our successes! That was a questionable way to celebrate the end of our agile activity! This intranet version lasted at our company for over a decade, as it was well-liked and well-received by our employees.

Communicating an end state to stakeholders up front would have solidified plans and defined the critical path. Having a user group to derive that end state would have avoided the scope creep that we suffered on this project.

There are many options for managing scope creep, including grooming the back log and identifying the definition of done. An organization change management plan would have drawn a line in the sand, and agreement with users would have gone a long way in marching towards that goal.

Get users involved and use an organizational change management plan to communicate goals to the organization.

The project's mission outcome was to improve employees' central access to corporate functions through exciting new features and technology to enhance their intranet experience. We did successfully achieve this outcome, though there were times on the project when priorities were not clear and too many user stories clouded our vision.

We should have developed an Organizational Change Management Plan to communicate the expected end state for the new intranet and minimize scope creep. This can be critical on an agile effort which boasts a major benefit of "learning as we go" — which can continue to swell that user story backlog and scope. Figure 8 shows an example of the steps in an organizational change management process.

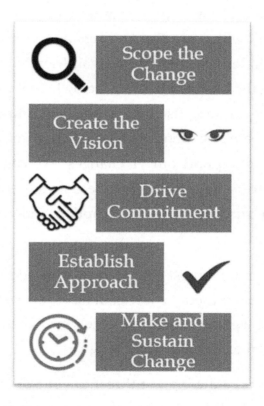

Figure 8. Example Organization Change Management Process

Organization change management (OCM) clarifies how the system will impact the human commitment. It clarifies that we are not doing this *to you*, we are doing this *for you*, with you, and on your behalf. The OCM curve varies from those eager participants who are early adopters to those who will do as they are told and those resistors who will only do it "over their dead body." Your project needs to commit to moving your stakeholders up the OCM curve.

Although we didn't use this approach for this use case (though we should have), I have implemented change management on other projects with success. Our change management plan execution includes starting with a small friendly group of users and collecting their feedback. After seeing how it works for them, we gradually added users. As we continue the change management path, we identify experts within each organization to promote and support our IT changes. We convince our key stakeholders to be evangelists for the new system. We identify and collect metrics to track usage, adoption, and satisfaction with the new system.

Change is difficult for most people. As people adapted to the new intranet, our identified "cheerleaders," our support hotline, video training vignettes, and online help provided the necessary support needed to ease into the change.

Scope creep can be the biggest threat to your project in terms of lengthening schedule, increasing cost, and lowering your chances of success. It happens when features are added that were not in the original plan and unaccounted for in cost and schedule. Just learning to say "no" may not be enough to deter your stakeholders from wanting to add, enhance, and augment your original plans. Figure 9 presents some ways of avoiding scope creep. Document and clarify your scope upfront clearly and adhere to PM practices of managing your cost and schedule to that specific scope. Put any unrequested features in a separate phase to be considered after the first phase is completed, but don't add them to your initial release. Minimize gaps in any stakeholder communications and make decisions quickly without requiring the advice of others. Documenting the project change management plan and definition of "done" gives you guideposts to reach your successful mission outcome.

Figure 9. Ways to Avoid Scope Creep.

Once you know the eventual goals and business results, stakeholders need to understand how you plan to get there. In this case, we used an electronic Kanban board to track the tasks for each sprint.

A Kanban board manages work by visually depicting work at various stages of a process using cards to represent work items and columns to represent each stage of the process. We used a Kanban board to manage our agile project, starting out with a white board with actual index cards taped to the board. By the end of the effort, we had automated the board to include remote team members. Figure 10 shows an example Kanban board, showing sticky notes representing tangible or online cards indicating tasks with accompanying detail.

Figure 10. Example Kanban Board

Our team benefitted by its ease of use, visual interface, and ability to see what everyone was working on. At our daily standup meetings, we gathered around the Kanban board so that team members could choose their next tasks or move items into the next phase. PMs can assign work when a team member is idle. The process facilitates the movement of work from the user story backlog to the To-Do column, into the In-Process column, and then to In-Test, and finally into the Done column. The cards can be comprised of added details such as who is assigned, how long it will take to complete, and any dependent tasks.

In our project, we defined several epic stories — those that are so large that they comprise multiple sub-tasks or stories within them. For example, we had defined a news story epic that included several sub-tasks such as corporate news, customizable news feeds, and organization news feeds. Testing an epic is dependent on the remaining sub-items for the testing to be completed. Increased communication is one of the best benefits of an agile approach, with both team members and stakeholders. The Kanban board is a tool that helps with that communication.

Some of our team members were reluctant to move to agile methodology, even though they had been trained in the new approach. This resulted in a team of diverse thinkers.

Leadership of diverse teams with different approaches and definitions of success means you need to make room for confusion, conflict, and disagreement. Many on our team were used to doing waterfall development and felt uncomfortable in a strange new environment where they believed that everyone thought differently. Other frequent thoughts included "I am in the minority in my thinking and in my habits," "I do not have the right skills for this job," "I am second-guessing myself," and "I am not reaching out appropriately." Once you determine that you have a diverse team, whether in thought or culture, the next step is for you to make the team feel inclusive and ensure that all thoughts are welcomed and encouraged.

The more diverse the team, the better and richer the results will be, based on my experience with a variety of staff supporting projects. There are no stupid questions, and everyone is welcome and supported in their ideas. To foster diversity, establish a regular "touch base" with team members to build trust as you eliminate blockers and minimize friction that can slow achieving success. Build loyalty and agreement through group thinking and build their confidence.

There are other ways to ensure you are encouraging your diverse team of thinkers. Engage with the team to make all employees feel valued and be sure to take on other people's challenges to help them through a set of solutions. Be aware that minority employees might think they are not represented well or feel excluded. Give people the opportunity to speak up in many different settings. Support team members who struggle with their ability to be heard: typically, they are unlike most of the team, such as women and minorities.

Another way to enhance diversity and inclusion on your team is to standardize the interview process when hiring new employees. All applicants should get the same questions in order to level the playing field and encourage a variety of applicants. Be sure that your interview team is also diverse and inclusive to ensure that the questions represent that diversity.

Summary

Keeping stakeholders informed is one of the best features of agile since that step is regularly scheduled during sprint reviews. Minimize scope creep by defining a critical path to the project's end state. This will enhance your chances of meeting project goals in terms of both schedule and resources. Using tools such as Kanban boards and Organizational Change Management Plans can also ensure that stakeholders know the project's end state and how you plan to get there. The agile methodology can create a team of diverse thinking. This leads to assembling diverse and inclusive teams, which are beneficial due to the variety of ideas and thoughts that lead to success. Support that inclusivity and you will see your success rate soar.

PMs must provide status updates to stakeholders, which can take time and energy to create. However, spending too much time on these administrative tasks can be detrimental, as we will soon see in our next case study.

CHECKLIST

Executing - Moving it Along

Moving it Along: Execute project, manage tasks, delegate work, ensure the team is following the plan

✓ Conduct requirements and design reviews

✓ Run meetings with specific agendas resulting in detailed action items

✓ Consider using agile methodology, which includes short-duration sprints with daily standup meetings to encourage gradual implementation and continual learning

✓ Avoid scope creep by grooming user story backlog and have a definition of "done"

✓ Planning – communications, training, UAT, testing, organizational change management

✓ Build agile, inclusive, and diverse teams by encouraging communication, group thinking, support introverts, providing mentorship, and building on individual strengths

✓ Define metrics to measure success and collect baseline metrics on the As-Is system

Tools and techniques

✓ Continue to update schedule, budget, requirements, and user stories

✓ Define epic stories – large enough to comprise several sub-tasks or stories within them

✓ Execute using Kanban boards to organize work into To-Do, In-Progress, and Done

✓ Become effective at visually depicting work at various stages of process using cards to represent work items and columns to represent stages of the process: To-Do, In-Progress, In-Test, Done.

✓ Define change management plan to communicate expected end state and to minimize scope creep

✓ Use diagramming to refine processes, data flows, and governance decisions, including Venn diagrams, journey maps and others

Soft skills: Demonstrate decision-making by forcing issue resolution, exercise grace and respect, provide encouragement and assistance where needed, second-guess rationale for decisions to ensure they are the right ones

CHAPTER 5
MONITORING
What's Going On?

It is not the genius at the top giving directions that makes people great. It is great people that make the guy at the top look like a genius.

—Simon Sinek

I once read the wrong book for a book club — it had the correct title but it was written by a different author. It took me weeks to finish that book only to find out that I was working hard — but working wrong. Working on the right things is critical to maximizing your contribution to a project's success. Your relevance occurs when you are critical to the success of the project. You need to be irreplaceable, not irrelevant.

Project management relevance relies on execution, and this can be jeopardized by excessive stakeholder communication. You only have a limited amount of time, so you need to decide how to apportion that time appropriately. Being less administrative and more attentive to project goals and deliverables makes you irreplaceable.

This chapter will discuss how the PM communicates with stakeholders on status, goals, and budget. Other mechanisms for reporting on adoption and success consist of metrics and success measures to evaluate impact. The PM may be part of a Project Management Office (PMO), which is a group of PMs intended to drive project success by applying their collective expertise.

Stakeholder Communication is conducted regularly to indicate *what we have done, what we are working on,* and *what the blockers to success are.* This is a critical PM deliverable to ensure that what you are working on meets the stakeholder's anticipated needs.

Metrics or Success Measures are areas where you can quantify the project success. Collecting metrics data proves where your work has made a successful impact. Being fully embedded with the project outcomes and goals helps you to define metrics.

Project Management Office (PMO) is a group of PMs who can be assigned to provide direct PM support. These PMs are embedded with the project and devote their attention to reporting, goals, and deliverables.

Characteristics exhibited during this phase include communicating regularly with stakeholders, being aware of environment, ensuring tasks are on schedule, believing in your project, and demonstrating your passion for its success!

The PM should be embedded into the project in order to demonstrate value and drive it forward. This use case will illustrate why you should be less administrative and more attentive to project goals.

CASE STUDY

Maximize project involvement to avoid getting replaced

There are PM skills that can make you a critical team member. If PMs are not driving project success, then they risk becoming irrelevant. Just doing schedules and status reports is not adequate for running a project as a PM. You need to find a way to be a critical team member.

To manage a multi-year, multi-system rollout, management hired a half-dozen PMs to form a centralized Project Management Office (PMO). This group reported to stakeholders on portfolio schedules, status, and risk. Asking each team for a weekly update, the PMO reported to the Steering Committee. The PMO got caught up in reporting and didn't focus enough on delivery. After six months, the entire staff in the PMO was replaced.

As the business analyst on the Human Capital Management vendor selection team, I worked on one of the projects within this portfolio. Each project had its own separate PM that managed the delivery, and these PMs were not part of the overall PMO. Those in the PMO acted as an additional set of PMs whose job it was to report on status. This PMO coordinated weekly meetings and gathered information from standardized reports on accomplishments and plans. They coordinated regular steering committee review meetings, budgets, and milestones.

As a PM, you can't just run meetings and do status reports — you must focus on execution and become integral to success or your work will not be valued. The PMO should have created a bridge to the business and tried to quantify the mission impact, including addressing cross-functional issues. The portfolio was complex because it consisted of five vendor products, representing millions of dollars in investment, all with different customers (e.g., finance, HR, contracts, travel, and portfolio management).

63

This portfolio replaced existing old technology with new, often utilizing cloud-based software solutions, requiring schedule coordination and data integrations across platforms.

Even after the PMO was replaced, people worried about the health of the project. Some in the PMO were talented PMs with years of experience and extremely valuable skills. We worried about our friends who were impacted and how they would land on their feet (they all did, I am very happy to report). We were unhappy with the change that occurred, but as a PM, I needed to be cautious about how emotionally attached to the project I became, since I had to help manage the change.

My department has an IT PMO that is separate from the one mentioned in this use case. My PMO is responsible for the success of individual IT projects within the organization, and each PM is assigned three to five projects. We strive as managers to ensure that all our PMO members are assigned to critical IT projects, making sure that they are relevant and crucial members of the organization.

How many times have you been in status meetings when everyone says that everything is fine, even though you have heard from others on the effort that things are not fine at all? Even when you do what you are told (and do it well, by the way), it may not be enough. To be fair, the world of IT project management can indeed be shaky ground if the project managers are not critical to project delivery. Our jobs may not really be in danger, but we can imagine that they are — and, oh, how we do that. You need to have confidence in your role, knowing the key processes and how you are adding value. Rather than feeling threatened and hoarding information in a defensive posture, ensure that collaborative decisions are being made and work is being performed.

Be a critical team player by getting deep enough into the project to understand the outcomes such that you can quantify them using metrics for program success measures. There are other ways to be a critical team member including managing cross-coordination issues across multiple efforts, identifying and driving data integration issues, as well as communicating cross-functional impacts with stakeholders.

You can assure the individual project team's success by developing success measures and metrics.

The PMO's mission outcome was to provide stakeholder communication, such as cross-functional planning. The PMO satisfied the stakeholder communication but did not have emphasis on cross-functional planning. Replacing the PMO and focusing on cross-system issues achieved the mission outcomes.

The PMO should have had a focus on the project portfolio business outcomes and worked across the projects to highlight cross-functional issues, such as data integrations. To be a highly sought-after and necessary asset, the PM needs to take ownership in order to execute on key issues, to be a leader, and to be the go-to person. You cannot define success measures unless you are intimately familiar with a project. Figure 11 shows an example of metrics that includes user adoption and customer satisfaction.

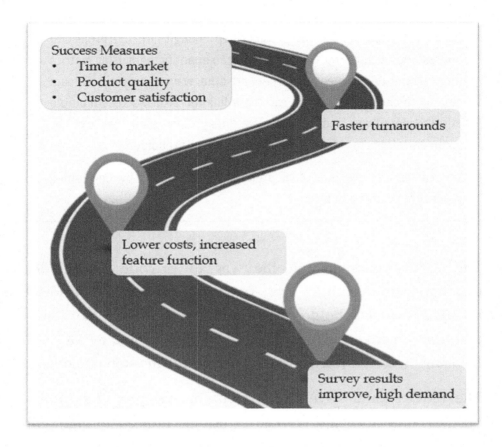

Figure 11. Success Measures or Metrics

Metrics such as these can help teams feel more connected to their work and help stakeholders better understand the value proposition. Business outcomes are the intangible results and the human aspect of your project success. These can provide direction and incentive for your team.

Business outcomes are often a bridge to the business to quantify the mission impact, including cross-functional issues. You should align identification of intended business outcomes early during project start up in order to increase your potential for success. Six good questions to ask are:

1. What are the data-driven technical products that your team will produce?

2. What are the actionable recommendations?

3. What timely stakeholder decisions need to be made that you will influence?

4. What are the business drivers and the mission outcomes?

5. How will success be measured?

6. What are the measurable business outcomes?

It is often hard to come up with quantitative and measurable metrics to quantify the success of your project. Often, they are related to adoption of the new system, the value of the gaps that have been closed, and overall user satisfaction. Adoption can be automatically established via tracking software. Other identified measures can be gathered through surveys and interviews with new users, but these are hard to quantify and determine a range within which you hope to achieve results. This is one of the many ways that PMs can start to become irreplaceable, rather than irrelevant.

When your manager asks for status reports, be sure that is not the only thing you do. You need to find the right level of detail to satisfy stakeholders while also allowing time for you to focus on project success. Status reports are timely updates on the project's progress, and they help address risks and issues on the minds of stakeholders. Written concisely, they offer high-level information, rather than focusing on every detail. Figure 12 shows a sample status report that includes schedule, function, risks, and budget information.

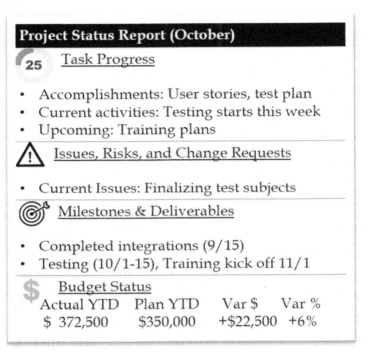

Figure 12. Example Status Report

As an overall view, you want to state your accomplishments in the past as well as your next steps. Aligned with your Work Breakdown Structure, you should indicate recent and upcoming milestones and your status using a percentage. You should also point out any risks or blockers that need to be mitigated. Summary budget status tracks planned vs. actual costs and indicates spending trends for stakeholder review. These should be reported in a regular cadence, such as every two to four weeks. If your stakeholders need regular updates but don't have time to attend status meetings, then you should send a brief emailed status report.

In my experience, stakeholder communication requires a formula that is repeatable, consistent, and regular. In some cases, I have included links to other documents, such as the schedule or project charter. And above all, I suggest that you keep it at a high level so it is neither difficult to create nor overwhelming to read.

In our case study, the group of project managers who formed the PMO worked for a portfolio of specific work that represents a huge investment in new commercial software products. There are other ways to introduce a PMO into the organization to supply PMs to projects to drive success.

Running an IT PMO is different than a PMO that is dedicated to a specific project. The IT PMO that I manage in my department was formed to specifically run projects in IT, and each PM is often assigned to between three and five projects each. Not only do they communicate with stakeholders, but they also help the effort to be successful, and are often critical to driving the project forward.

Our IT PMO consists of six to eight PMs whose job it is to drive project complexity on a myriad of IT projects ranging in technology from infrastructure to cyber security to HR to contracts. In each case, they apply their PM skills to organize, focus, structure, and drive the work as the leader, spokesperson, and key player on the project. We focus less on administrative and documentation details and more on working shoulder-to-shoulder with engineers whose talents lie in technology so that we can organize and drive execution to deliver success.

We have a list of requests that we prioritize for the PMO to support the highest priority projects in the organization. Some examples of work we have done include running a vendor purchase for acquisition of new products, requirements definition and schedules, managing Kanban boards for running tasks, executing test programs, managing budgets for resources, coordinating across organizations, putting together project charters, defining business cases, giving product demos, and being a trusted advisor on the project.

Our IT PMO has assisted the organization in establishing a top-ten prioritized list of projects that is updated monthly. In this way, we can focus our attention on delivering on those 10 projects, and our PMO typically is a critical player in these efforts. We have also been involved in resource management, portfolio management, budgets, sustainment, and service manager definitions. Our stakeholder reviews consist of quarterly director reviews, bi-monthly CIO reviews, and regular check-ins with the business unit managers. These business outcome managers are responsible for understanding our customer's needs and working those into our budget plan to ensure that we are delivering on their highest priorities.

There are three different types of project managers: supportive, controlling, and directive. We tend to do a combination of controlling and directive project support.

- Supportive: Provides a consultative role to projects by supplying templates, best practices, access to information and lessons learned from previous projects;

- Controlling: Provides support and becomes a team member;

- Directive: Provides direct control of projects by directly executing them.

In our case study, the PMO was originally set up to be directive and gradually over time became supportive, which is one of the reasons why they were reassigned. They failed to focus on delivery and driving decisions and instead were performing the roll of project coordinators. In addition, the PMO suffered from growing too big too fast, which resulted in top-heavy management and slow decision-making skills.

Summary

PMs should provide stakeholder communication — in moderation. Your primary job is to drive project complexity, using lightweight reporting and heavyweight project support. One example of a tool you can use is to create success measures or metrics, which require that you have project familiarity. Use a streamlined template for your status report, keep it at a high level, and identify near-term schedule items. There are ways to run a successful PMO, executing on projects and providing minimal stakeholder communication.

Now that you have established your status review cadence with stakeholders, your focus should turn to potential users to assess their satisfaction with your project. Will they be delighted and find your project useful?

CHECKLIST

Monitoring - What's Going On

What's Going On: Report status to stakeholders, including budget and schedule

✓ Conduct regular stakeholder reviews on status to be comprised of accomplishments, what we are doing next, any barriers to execution

✓ Communicate with stakeholders, prepare answers for questions from executives

✓ Become the expert on the product, give the demos, answer all the questions

✓ Be a critical team member, take ownership to execute on key project issues, be the go-to person on the project

✓ Run a successful PMO by embedding PMs with projects to organize, focus, structure, and drive the work as a key player

✓ Focus less on administrative and documentation details, pay more attention to project goals and deliverables

✓ Be irreplaceable, not irrelevant

Tools and techniques

✓ Continue to update schedule, budget, requirements, and user stories

---

✓ Generate template-based status reports that update high-level progress, such as accomplishments, plans, and key milestones with percentage complete

✓ Define success measures to quantify system adoption, improvements to the business, gaps that have been closed, cost savings, and user satisfaction

✓ Develop business outcomes that define data-driven technical products, actionable recommendations, timely stakeholder decisions, business drivers and mission outcomes

Soft skills: Communicate with stakeholders, be aware of environment, make sure things are on schedule, believe in your project and demonstrate your passion for its success

CHAPTER 6
MONITORING
Do We Like It?

If you don't set your own agenda, somebody else will... If I didn't fill my schedule with things I felt were important, other people would fill my schedule with things they felt were important.

— Melinda Gates

As the lead singer in my band, I have accidentally missed lyrics and skipped verses hoping the audience didn't notice — but my bandmates always noticed. Users can be somewhat like band members in that they are typically demanding people with high expectations who would rather criticize than applaud your efforts. Getting users involved early can be risky because they may want to dictate your approach and be critical if you choose not to follow their recommendations.

Of course, we all think we know best so why would we need to consult with users at all? Well, what happens when user dissatisfaction results in an unacceptable product? I guarantee you that it can get ugly!

This chapter will discuss how the PM interacts with users to ensure their satisfaction. Defining user personas can drive awareness of the pains and opportunities currently experienced. Conducting user acceptance testing (UAT) walks users through your system to gather their feedback and suggested changes. In continuing to align your staff plan, you may need to shift resources on or off your project, depending on budget and project needs.

Personas are detailed descriptions of users who will need to access your system. They identify their role, their key use cases, and their specific pain points and opportunities for improvement.

User Acceptance Testing (UAT) is a series of tests intended to gather user feedback. Just offering lip service to users is not enough. Just recording their worries and putting them on a shelf is also not enough. Critical analysis of their concerns and evaluation of whether they should be heeded — that is the recipe for success.

Resource monitoring is the process by which managers monitor and determine assignments of staff to work, based on project funding, staff availability, and skill matching.

Characteristics exhibited during this phase include integrity, working with users, agility, dependability, trustworthy, authentic, giving direction, accepting feedback, and reporting on user commentary.

To ensure awareness about proposed users who will be test subjects, analyzing their traits can predict their pains and focus the UAT in the right areas. This use case will illustrate why it is important to analyze your user's biggest pain points.

CASE STUDY

Tend to user needs to avoid getting project put on hold

After demonstrating our final configuration of our software product, our stakeholders had reservations about a new feature that users did not like. Generally, you want to delight your users, especially when swapping out an old system for a new one. Your hope is that the new system will be better than the existing one.

This project was focused on replacing an existing HR performance management system, used by 8,000 employees, for annual performance evaluations and salary increases. We selected a vendor after months of analysis, purchased the product, and configured the product to HR's stated requirements. We conducted user acceptance testing (UAT), during which users expressed concerns about the newly added employee scoring system. Stakeholders put the whole project on hold until we reconfigured the product to remove the scoring feature.

As the project manager, I ran the UAT and wrote the UAT test plans. However, UAT was conducted too late in the schedule to impact any major changes. Had we gathered their views earlier, we might have discovered the problematic issues sooner. In this case, UAT was more of a proverbial rubber stamp than an actual gathering of real user feedback. And, boy, did they make their feelings known! Complexity factors that impacted this project included the following: it was the company's first cloud product; the new compensation system was replacing an effective, well-known, and cherished custom-built tool; we were adding new rating scores; and security issues had to be addressed. In hindsight, there were a ton of potential issues.

On a gray day in March, the project team presented the new HR commercial product that would change every employee's life once a year. Little did we know that this demo would be the reason our rollout was put on hold for a year. What did the users think of the new system? We had to admit that we had heard some concerns.

Luckily, we had executed user acceptance testing in the prior month. Nonetheless, users were uncomfortable with the new employee scoring module, which was not required by the tool, but was a handy new feature that was industry best practice. After all, this change was a big reason why we chose this product in the first place. We argued that users would get used to it and in the end would see its value. Users were concerned that the scoring module could be interpreted differently by employees, and there were concerns that inconsistencies would upset the staff.

There is a philosophy that says a critical evaluator involves policy and guidance, which could include anything that might disrupt employees with a significant change. Policy evaluation should be part of any review and communicated to stakeholders. This employee scoring module is an example of a policy change that clearly required approval of an authoritative individual, board, or committee prior to launching. We didn't recognize this until it was already implemented and then had to be removed.

After the demo was over, we had the impression that all had gone well. Then we heard the project was being put on hold due to the need to conduct a corporate review of the new feature. HR conducted focus group assessments to determine how to best reconfigure the system to remove the scoring function. By the time it moved to an operational capability, a year had gone by since that fateful demonstration day.

Other questions that we were asked included, did we get the most out of the vendor product that we could possibly get? Did it transform the business rather than just being a 1:1 replacement of an old system? We are often asked to keep in mind the bigger picture, not just meet the detailed requirements. From a strategic viewpoint, did we achieve the overall goal of business transformation? Our answer was "yes."

Although we drove the project to success, the outcome was delayed. In fact, this new performance management system remained in production for about eight years before it was replaced. As a company, we have changed the way we do performance management many times, and the cloud systems allow for flexibility to configure multiple approaches. In our case, users were not consulted soon enough to impact the design and implementation.

In a consulting organization, resource monitoring and utilization were key factors in determining whether we would lose key resources on the project. As my time on this effort became less important and UAT changes caused project delays, I was reassigned to a new activity while the HR team the reconfiguration. Our IT staff members are frequently requested to support the business, such as HR or Finance or Contracts, to help with a variety of their efforts. We track these requests as our opportunity pipeline, and as staff move off activities, we assign those with the right skills to these new assignments.

In summary, you can avoid project delays by ensuring early user involvement in order to vet their opinions and leave time to incorporate suggestions. It helps to evaluate the overall makeup of your test subjects and specific pain points you plan to review during the UAT event.

There are many ways to focus on user issues and pain points, such as creating user scripts, interviewing users, and demonstrations. In each of these cases, persona analysis can pinpoint the differentiators to ensure that you maximize the user's time.

Do persona analysis to analyze the users' greatest pain points and be sure UAT emphasizes those areas.

The project's mission outcome was to provide an enhanced user experience for their annual performance management and salary adjustment tool features, on time. We didn't hit that date, but it was eventually rolled out with success.

The case study illustrates the need to examine user concerns with the As-Is system in order to ensure that the To-Be system will adequately address their needs. By highlighting the employee scoring feature, we could have obtained important feedback and removed or modified that feature accordingly. In our situation, people managers needed to write staff reviews and then identify any nuances unique to the current system. Figure 13 shows a persona example of a people manager with key issues enumerated as that role relates to our specific project.

People Manager
Key User Stories
As a People Manager:
- I need to write staff performance reviews annually
- I would benefit from the insights of other managers
- I need a way to compare my staff against others

Pain Points / Opportunities	Unique to Current System
• No standard way to compare staff against others • People get concerned when they are scored using numbers, due to possible misinterpretation	• No scoring in built into system • Managers create their own scoring system but do not share with staff

Figure 13. Sample Persona

By documenting our perception of a people manager, we used this to review with an actual set of people managers to ensure we had it right and focused on the main issues. In my experience, we have developed persona cards to represent different users, such as an employee and a manager. As part of the persona card, we highlight the scoring system or any other functions that we want to examine more deeply. We validate these assumptions directly with users prior to the UAT and adjust as needed. Then we validate our predictions with user testing.

Personas for our UAT program included employees (who create performance plans), administrators (who perform coordination), and HR staff (who turn on/off performance plans and run reports).

I think that personas are a great starting point for thinking about the needed journeys and use cases. One example of where personas have been useful was in developing a training plan. By identifying a separate swim lane for each persona, we focused training specifically for that user type and could clearly see their steps enumerated in that particular swim lane. Each persona can be responsible for executing very different tasks within the system, so the personas are helpful in identifying the key issues addressed by each user. Swim lanes, user stories, and test cases can all be tied to different personas.

In conducting our user acceptance test (UAT), we tried to answer the question: Have we produced the results that customers want? We needed both functional experts and business owners to run the UAT. Once the tests were completed, user comments and issues were documented in a report, a sample of which is shown in Figure 14.

Test Description [?]✓	Severity	Summary	Initial Test	Readiness Test	Production Test	Vendor Test	Assigned to
Network connection using new protocols	High	Ready	OK	Fail	Fail	OK	J. Doe
Rollback: Network using prior protocol	Med	Ready	OK	OK	OK	OK	A. Shu

Figure 14. Sample User Acceptance Test Results

82

The first step in conducting UAT is to identify your test subjects, which should include a sampling of a cross-section of users. The second step is to write a set of UAT test scripts, for example:

1. Verify that the employee can complete performance self-assessment, forward to next steps, receive notifications, and print performance appraisal

2. Verify that the manager can complete assessment and conduct salary recommendations in compensation module

The third step is to conduct the UAT with users, and there are 3 ways to do that:

1. Give them the scripts and ask them for their responses by a certain date

2. Schedule a time and walk them through the UAT, either individually or as a group

3. Roll out features to a select group of people and set up a communication channel for people to comment on their experience

The final steps are to prioritize and integrate test results. Talk with users and highlight their key concerns, talk to business owners about alternatives, incorporate change, re-visit UAT with users, and report any gaps.

Here are the steps and a typical timeline for a 12-month project: plan/scope UAT (month 2), design/execute UAT (month 4), track / prioritize issues (month 5), incorporate changes (month 6), review changes with users (month 8).

Given that our UAT was conducted too late, our project was put on hold to incorporate the changes. By then, I had been reassigned to a new effort, thanks to our extensive resource monitoring team.

Managing a group of people comes with its own challenges, like the need to make sure they have high priority projects to support that match their skill areas. We have a system in place by which we track capacity and demand management, prioritizing the high value work and assigning individuals with the appropriate skills. Our staff is counting on us to find the right work for them, including challenging and satisfactory work programs. We try to keep our most valuable assets productive and happy with solid assignments that provide leadership potential. If we have resources that are in short supply, we steer our hiring plan in that direction, or we place staff in training programs.

As a consultant, we have options for placing our staff on projects. The main desire behind every request is to assign a PM to the project as a direct contributor and team member. If we are short on resources, then we might take a different approach and assign an individual as a reviewer, when they are asked to fix a project that may have some issues. This is a shorter term, but more intense assignment whereby the team may re-structure the project or make other recommendations. Another alternative would be to assign someone as an advisor and meet with the team in some regular cadence (e.g., weekly) when they provide guidance and templates that can be helpful.

One of the main jobs of a resource manager is to conduct a performance management review for each direct report. In my experience, this is conducted at the end of the year, when each employee documents goals, work performed, and a self- rating. Resource managers write their own commentary on the employees' statements. Difficult conversations are usually the most successful when there is honest dialog throughout the year and there are no surprises. Supply and demand management can be better managed when staff are appropriately guided towards the right skill expertise.

Summary

Users should be delighted by the results of your project. Find out what resonates with users and fix problems that users have highlighted. It only makes sense that if you want to delight your users, then you need to include them in the process of building your new approach. It will be a win-win situation if everyone is happy with the results. Conducting UAT and analyzing your users with persona cards are great examples of ways to connect with users. And in our case, the UAT was all about performance management — one of the many responsibilities of the resource manager.

Once the users agree on your approach, you will need a test program to ensure the system is working correctly. In some cases, your project will not conduct a UAT, especially when there is no test environment available, such as a network upgrade. A general testing program is almost always needed, so let's take a look at what is involved in testing adequately for the needs of your project.

CHECKLIST

Monitoring - Do We Like It?

Do We Like It: Evaluate user and stakeholder level of confidence in solution

✓ Involve users early in order to minimize risk

✓ Conduct some form of user acceptance testing (UAT) to assess whether you will delight users with the new system.

✓ Conduct UAT planning, including identifying participants and setting up accounts

✓ Write test plan, review with team to ensure completeness

✓ Execute resource monitoring when new assignments need staff with appropriate skills, and initiate training when a skills mismatch occurs

Tools and techniques

✓ Use personas to document your perception of a type of person who will use your system, use those assumptions to review with an actual user of that type to confirm your suspicions, and perhaps highlight other things you had not thought of

✓ Validate persona issues to examine users' pains and opportunities, and highlight key new features

✓ Generate UAT use cases and test scripts

✓ Conduct UAT using three possible approaches: 1. give them scripts and expect responses by a certain date, 2. schedule time and walk through UAT, 3. roll out features to select group and provide communication channel for feedback

✓ Prioritize results, highlight key issues, derive alternatives, incorporate changes, and re-do UAT

✓ Leave enough time to incorporate changes and re-run UAT

✓ UAT test results: Analyze user concerns and evaluate whether they should be heeded

Soft skills: Demonstrate integrity, working with users, eagerness, agility, dependability, trustworthy, authentic, giving direction accepting feedback, and reporting on user commentary

CHAPTER 7
CONTROLLING
Does it Work?

"When we work from a place that says I'm enough, then we stop screaming and start listening, we're kinder and gentler to the people around us and we're kinder and gentler to ourselves."

—Daring Greatly, by Brene Brown

While rushing through a shopping center, I once opened a door that hit me in the face, cutting my eyebrow badly enough to need seven stitches. That was obviously a careless mistake — and we can all make these kinds of mistakes including at work. You spent all night fixing your broken system? Just try explaining that to your stakeholders the next day!

It's normally risky to make significant changes since these can impact many downstream systems. Assuming that all will go well is never a good idea. I've been unsuccessful at moving to an operational system more times than I care to recall, so lessons learned about my challenges should help you avoid similar mistakes.

This chapter will discuss how the PM coordinates the test program to validate that the system meets the expected requirements. In preparing for moving to an operational system, conducting a "premortem exercise" can identify risks so you can plan mitigation tactics. Every rollout should have a contingency plan in place, including a well-documented rollback plan. Prior to rollout, the PM conducts a Change Readiness Review to give all stakeholders an opportunity to weigh in as to whether we are prepared for rollout.

Test program is a series of tests intended to exercise most, if not all, functionality of the system to ensure high quality. This consists of documenting test steps, gathering results, prioritizing problems, fixing any uncovered issues, and re-testing by using a sub-set of the tests, often called a smoke test.

Premortem exercise is when the team brainstorms all possible ways that a project plan can fail, and ways to mitigate those risks. This is particularly important in order to maintain risk management and resolution plans to minimize any negative impacts.

Rollout and Rollback Plans document steps to move your system to an operational environment and to reverse those steps in case something goes wrong. You worked hard to prepare for moving to an operational environment, and you want it to be successful. Testing the rollback approach is critical, especially when you are unable to test the rollout (e.g., a network upgrade).

Change Readiness Review is a meeting where stakeholders review materials (e.g., test results) to identify and evaluate the risks of your project rollout.

Characteristics exhibited during this phase include acceptance of a bumpy road, requiring a positive attitude, optimism, endurance, dexterity, and knowledge of governance, and being a team player

Risk management includes identifying risks and mitigation to prevent them. This use case will illustrate why it is important to prepare contingency plans in case challenges arise.

CASE STUDY

Plan for risk mitigation to avoid doing all night fix of erroneous changes

Moving your system to an operational environment with inadequate preparation is a recipe for disaster. A premortem exercise can predict risk areas and assist the team in preparing for their mitigation. No one wants to explain why the change had to be rolled back because of the problems it caused.

Under normal circumstances, significant test efforts precede the move of any system to an operational environment. On a weeknight, after hours, a network upgrade was put into place, and within a short time, this change caused the company's entire network to fail. The team spent the night rolling back the upgrade to a version of the configuration that was six-months old, since it was the only prior version they could find. The lack of contingency planning caused the team to have a rough night, but luckily the team was able to prevent an outage from occurring during business hours.

As the business analyst assigned to the project after the outage, I conducted a process analysis and lessons learned for the prevention of future occurrences of such issues.

Due to a myriad of technical challenges, the recovery of the downed network took too long. There was no PM in place prior to the rollout to ensure that testing or existence of any rollback was adequate. This network upgrade was needed to keep up with the vendor's timetable.

Due to the complexity of network architectures and rules, the network change was not well-understood and there was much trust placed in the vendor's recommendation to put the upgrade in place. One risk mitigator might have been to have vendor consulting available with a representative overnight but having experienced success with these types of rollouts in the past, the team felt that was unnecessary.

In the end, the network fixes were rolled back in an emergency overnight activity and few users were impacted. But this illustrates the concern over rolling errors into production and the angst that stakeholders can feel when these affect users, especially when they were avoidable had there been more preparation and risk mitigation in place.

If we had done a pre-mortem before this project even started, we might have been able to predict what happened. A pre-mortem exercise forces the team to think about all the ways the project can fail and put mitigation plans in place to avoid those risks. Preparing for challenges should be part of any move to an operational environment. Network upgrades are always risky because it is difficult to test their readiness. The team is forced to trust the vendor and hope the upgrade will not be disruptive.

In addition to risk prediction, all stakeholders should be involved in a change readiness review right before moving to an operational environment. During the meeting, the team goes around the room and asks everyone's opinion about whether we are ready to roll out.

As there was no PM assigned to this project, such a meeting was not conducted, as evidenced by the fact that there was no rollback plan. The Change Readiness Review would have certainly called for that, at a minimum. There might also be a need to potentially delay the change if there are still outstanding issues.

With most systems, prior to rollout we conduct an extensive test program. This includes writing scripts, tracking and prioritizing results, fixing problems, and re-testing. We use a test environment that is similar to production, but we don't test in production. We have a smoke test which is a short test of major functionality that we can execute in order to check or validate the move to production. The test team almost always finds problems in operational environment that were not caught in the test environment. For example, multiple people accessing the same data simultaneously may result in an error, and we cannot always check for that in the test environment.

I learned about these network change problems the next day, after the team had recovered and made the necessary fixes. It amazed me how many things went wrong that night, and more importantly, how amazingly smart the network team was to have recovered in the middle of the night, against all odds. I had to make sure I connected with all involved to get the right story in the documentation. I had to make sure I communicated with stakeholders on the issues so there was a clear picture and preparation for the next time, because I was assured there would certainly be a next time.

Things were not tested adequately. Also, there was no roll back plan if something were to go wrong. The most recent configuration the team could find was six months old, and no details were to be found with the networks all down. Most of the issues encountered were avoidable had better risk mitigation been in place.

We saw the critical importance of testing and of having a roll back plan. In reality, we have rolled back more times than we have not.

The team needs to huddle to think of possible ways that this move to an operational environment might fail. One way to do that is by conducting a pre-mortem at the beginning of the project. Other methods include brainstorming during which you list everyone's ideas and examine each one for relative merit. Other ways to predict failure consist of interviewing the vendor for their experiences and working with stakeholders to decide whether the organization is ready to accept the risk.

Do a pre-mortem during the project to predict and mitigate future risks.

The project's mission outcome was to successfully rollout network changes to keep up with the vendor's timetable without impact to other systems. This was unsuccessful, and the rollback was also unsuccessful, considering that it took all night. Had we done a pre-mortem and prepared for challenges to arise, we would have had a fallback plan in place.

We should have conducted a pre-mortem to predict the worst risks that could happen at the beginning of the effort and to identify risk mitigation to prevent its occurrence. A Change Readiness Review can assess those risk mitigators using a documented rollback plan. Figure 15 shows an example outline of a pre-mortem exercise.

Describe Failure ☹	Symptoms	List the Causes ☰
What important stuff did we not do?	How will we know we failed?	What did we do to cause failure?
What current problems remain?	If we don't do _____, it's a fail.	What did we not do to cause use to fail?
What new problems emerged?	If the only thing we do is _____, it's a win.	What incorrect assumptions did we make?

Figure 15. Example Outline of a Premortem

On one of my projects, the company hired an external consultant to motivate the team as they were about to embark on a major business transformation effort. He gave everyone two minutes to imagine the worst ending to our project and what might happen. Then we had twenty minutes to walk around and talk to others about what we had imagined. Then he gave us two minutes to come up with ways to prevent that from happening, and he again gave us twenty minutes to discuss this with others. Then we went around the room and each of us talked about the most important preventative measures on our list. It was an eye-opener for sure and helped in many stages of the project.

Once we have identified the risks from the pre-mortem, it's time to put those risk mitigation plans directly into the work program. For example, if you had detected in the pre-mortem that you might need a back-up in case you need to roll back the change, you would prepare that back-up. If you had detected in the pre-mortem that it would be helpful for the vendor to be online during the rollout to the operational environment, that could be arranged in advance. Most of the projects I've been on would benefit from a pre-mortem exercise, especially by asking the questions: How might this project fail and what are our avoidance tactics? Who would not want to know what to avoid and how to achieve a successful outcome?

Using these risk areas, one can easily transition into a Change Readiness Review, which is conducted just prior to the move to an operational environment. What risks might occur, and have we mitigated those risks properly?

A change readiness review is scheduled right before you move your system to production to ensure that all stakeholders agree that the team is ready based on the artifacts that have been presented. Figure 16 shows some examples of the questions that should be addressed during a change readiness review.

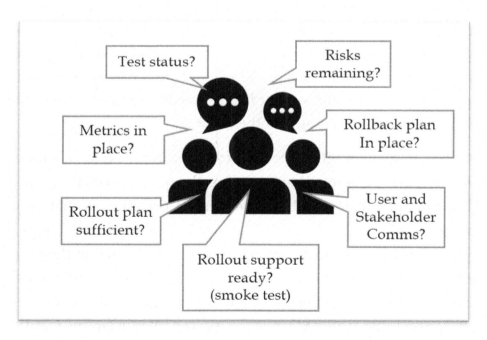

Figure 16. Example Change Readiness Review Data

I have conducted many change readiness reviews – some that have resulted in postponing our rollout. In my experience, some reasons for a delayed rollout have been comprised of the fact that we didn't have a rollback plan in place, the project still had significant test issues, or the plan would take too long to rollout. The change readiness review is conducted after you have completed a successful test program and your stakeholders agree that you're ready to operationalize your change. You can rollout with known errors, especially if they impact a small number of users, or if your issue happens infrequently (e.g., a printing error).

Typical questions that need to be asked include: Have you communicated to stakeholders and users? Are there risks remaining? and Have you adequately tested and incorporated final changes? Your stakeholders will assess your team's confidence and decide on the plan going forward.

During the test program, all hands are on deck to try to test as much of the system as possible. And if your uncovered test results only affects certain users, such as only the HR administrators, then there probably can be a rollout with the known problem. Be sure to alert that relatively small group to the issues, while the rest of the organization obtains the benefits of the new system. Rollouts with known issues where 95% of the system is working are common, as long as the known issues are communicated to stakeholders.

Rollout support should include representatives from the business, stakeholders, and functional leads. After the rollout, support should be put in place for users in case they have a problem. We have had success with our Corporate Help Desk, but also have set up chat or email with experts who are ready to answer questions.

You will want to be confident that the test program was executed as part of your Change Readiness Review. Testing is a critical function. Most projects run a test program prior to moving to an operational environment, although certain projects cannot easily be tested (e.g., network changes). The steps for running a test program consist of writing a test plan, writing test scripts, identifying testers, conducting the test, prioritizing issues, fixing issues, and re-testing. A smoke test is a high-level test that randomly checks one or two items in every piece of the system. These random tests provide some level of confidence that the whole system will work as planned. Smoke tests are usually conducted after the rollout to ensure that changes did not break other key functions.

The test plan includes information about what, when, and how you will conduct your test program. Test scripts typically take the form of a spreadsheet that indicates user type, action, expected result, actual result, and comments. For example, a step in a test could be the action to fill out a job application for a user type of employee. The expected result and the actual result could potentially compare the two, while the comments give the testers a place to write notes about that step.

In my experience with conducting test programs, we generally incorporate a wide variety of users from the business, customers, and users. In particular, we like to incorporate what we call "cowboys," who are the heaviest users of the system. The cowboys can point out edge cases — real-life examples that we may not have considered for testing.

Your test program should incorporate executing the test scripts with a variety of users, then collecting feedback and prioritizing the detected issues, and then identifying each issue with a high, medium, or low rating. For example, in one test program for which I was the PM, we had 20 different people in a room for two days. We walked them through the test scripts and helped as they executed the test. This was beneficial because they had no training and had trouble logging in. Sometimes we have had to conduct an end-to-end test, in which we put in data, waited a period of time for data to arrive in the right place, grabbed the data, and then validated that it had shown up in the right place. In this case, we needed multiple people to synchronize the test over time.

Identifying resources for the test program is critically important. Who will be responsible? What are the highest priority issues? What are risks if you do not execute on time? Are you using a tool to track test results, or are you doing it with a simple spreadsheet? Who is in charge and is it sharable with the team? Who is making the call on prioritization? You need to re-test the items that were fixed in order to ensure that they really have been fixed and didn't break something else. You should consider using a smoke test to quickly spot-check other aspects of the system.

Summary

No one wants to be up all night fixing problems, so you need to anticipate that this might happen and put things in place to mitigate that risk. The PM needs to clearly define the changes being made as well as any new features. A pre-mortem exercise can identify risks and put mitigation in place early, which would include setting up a rollback plan. A Change Readiness Review can assist stakeholders in deciding whether the team is ready to move to an operational environment, based on the current test and communication status. A test program validates that the change is ready and identifies any outstanding issues.

It is great to complete this major testing milestone to prepare for the final steps in the project. However, what if your project never ends? You will see what happens in the next chapter when no completion point is defined.

CHECKLIST

Controlling - Does it Work?

Does it Work? Execute test program, prioritize results

✓ Conduct a pre-mortem to predict how this project might fail and what the risk mitigation plans are that you can put into place to prevent these from occurring

✓ Run the test program to validate that your system works as expected

---

✓ Conduct test planning that includes who will be involved, what will be tested, when it will take place, and how you will conduct testing

✓ Execute the test with a wide variety of users, including edge cases. You might need an end-to-end test, where data is needed from another system. You may need to wait for data to be integrated, and then take steps to ensure that data ended up in the right place. Synchronize the test over time.

✓ Create a smoke test to check subsets of functionality in every area in order to gain confidence in a short test that can validate that it still works

✓ Conduct a change-readiness review with all stakeholders to ensure agreement that the project is ready to move to an operational system, based on presented artifacts

Tools and techniques

✓ Define test scripts, usually in the form of a spreadsheet indicating user type, action, expected result, actual result, and comments

✓ Identify testers, conduct a test, prioritize issues, fix issues, re-run the test using smoke test

✓ Run sample training on testing, as needed, in order to prepare testers

✓ Conduct testing to address functional areas, as well as performance testing and multiple device testing

✓ Review test results summary, report results to stakeholders, prioritize and analyze

✓ Prepare for contingencies and put the rollback plan in place prior to moving to operational environment

Soft skills: Bumpy road through this phase of testing, positive attitude, optimistic, endurance, dexterity, and knowledge of governance, and be a team player

CHAPTER 8
CONTROLLING
Are We Done Yet?

Spoken empathy most often comes in the form of statements that demonstrate that you have heard and understood the world of another…. When said from the heart, "that makes sense" is a powerful expression of validation.

—The Trusted Advisor Field Book

When my car needed a new muffler, timing belt, and transmission, I knew that it was time to replace it. Enough was enough. Too much money had been spent already. Similarly, in projects that seem to never end, it may be time to assign the team to something else. Projects can last a long time — sometimes too long. When is the right time to end it? Perhaps it should end when the mission outcome is realized.

The PM devises a rollout strategy to ensure protocol is followed and the system is ready to go. Otherwise, managers can question why you are continuing to add enhancements, when in fact they thought you were done already.

This chapter will discuss how the PM plans for the end of the project. Any outstanding features that are still needed can be diagrammed (e.g., workflow diagrams). Lessons Learned documents the good and bad elements for future use. Task force teams can be established to perform an independent assessment and recommend next steps.

Workflow Diagrams are created to illustrate the movement of how a system item flows through the process. This is drawn through the eyes of the user and can often help depict nuances in the project to determine whether a new feature should be added.

Task Force Teams are a set of independent experts called in to provide an assessment of the plans, schedule, features, and future plans.

Lesson Learned is a meeting of project staff to review and document what was done right and what could have been done better on the implementation. It is intended for reuse for future similar work.

Characteristics exhibited during this phase include dedication to putting out fires, dedication to the project's success, and not taking business decisions personally.

Having a known timetable for completing your project means that you have a specified set of goals with clear business outcomes. This use case will illustrate why it is important to define the project ending and not continually add features.

CASE STUDY

Define the end state to avoid project that never ends

Automating the travel expense process left us with a project that didn't have a specific end. We kept adding features until the stakeholders finally stopped the project. If we had used better tools to explain from a user's standpoint why certain features were needed, then we might have had less pushback from the stakeholders. No one wants to have their steps questioned, and the team wants a common understanding of necessary features from the business.

For a company whose employees travel a lot, we completed paper forms and got cash advances to track and audit travel expenses. Moving from a paper-based system to an online approach is always a challenge. We decided to build our own custom, trip-based, travel expense system, after ruling out a commercial product solution. This project lasted several years, as we continued to add features, like audit capabilities, auto-feed to financials for direct payment to payroll, and business rules around government daily allowances. As we continued this journey, we added foreign travel, which was not a feature of the original plan and which came under scrutiny by our stakeholders. They kept asking when the project would end.

I was the project manager of this development team and drove the work from conception to implementation to test and delivery. Our customer wanted foreign travel, which ended up being a successful implementation. However, we came up against resistance to proceed due to stakeholders thinking that we should be finished with the project. The new travel expense system exhibited many complexities such as business rules, audit restrictions, a small custom development team, and accelerated time to get reimbursement to payroll.

In addition, a whole piece of the project was dedicated to giving the audit team the ability to edit all expense reports.

Our initial rollout was not well-received because users questioned its fundamental functionality. The system started out with a basic form to print and sign/retrieve, with some basic error-checking. Then we added some database queries, business rules, auto-payment, and the ever-popular audit capability. Over time, we gradually added new features to make it a fully robust, custom-built travel expense system that catered to both the traveler and the travel office auditors' needs.

Part way through development, the company kicked off a two-day off-site travel review. Stakeholders and travelers gathered to identify ways to improve the end-to-end process, from booking to expensing trips. At that meeting, my customer's manager tasked me with certain actions instead of my customer — and as a result, she was offended by this slight and took it out on me.

I was disappointed that she was upset with me, and so I asked my manager if she could just do the tasking instead of me. She advised me not to take work decisions personally and reminded me that I was here to do a job. We are told what to do and even though we might not like it, we must still do it.

That was the best advice I ever received from my manager and mentor, and I have repeated it many times to my staff. We did eventually make up and resolve our issues and continued to work together for five years while this application was enhanced and modified. Within a few years of implementation, our travel expense system became popular as we added more useful features.

Up until that point, we had only catered to domestic travelers, so it was time to investigate whether we should add foreign travel, which has different rules than domestic travel. We defined the foreign travel requirements, which included, for example, modified business rules regarding reimbursement for hotel taxes.

Our stakeholders felt the investment in adding this functionality was not worth it for the small number (less than 25%) of travelers who go to foreign countries. But foreign travel expenses tend to be higher ticket items than those for domestic travel. We ended up proceeding with the implementation of foreign travel, completing it in less time than expected, and our foreign travelers were happy.

Having confidence in the product and knowing our way around adding enhancements, it was a natural next step for us to add foreign travel, even though our stakeholders disagreed. Workflow diagrams helped to explain from the user's standpoint why we needed to add foreign travel. The system, including foreign travel support, ended up being in place for over 20 successful years.

Projects can seem to go on forever for a variety of reasons, whether it be adding new functionality or different data feeds or different users. However, there needs to be an exit plan, with some understanding of when the project should end.

In our case, we had a cycle of development/rollout that was difficult to turn off, given that our team was not ready to end this cycle of success. The team had been together on this project for years, with no plan to halt adding features and supporting the travel office. But, we needed to have a plan in place that defined when we were done — whether when the project ran out of money or after we had finished a particular feature or after our customer was satisfied with any metrics that we could have defined.

Instead, our project ended abruptly when stakeholders decided *they* were done, and there was disappointment in being unable to continue adding further enhancements.

This project was the best team I have ever worked with. When you have a great team, you just mesh well with one another, and there is nothing like working with such a team that. We communicated well, had clear roles, jointly suggested solutions, and genuinely liked each other. We all knew our roles, helped each other along, and felt inspired by our efforts. The work itself was rewarding and we knew people liked what we were doing.

We almost gave the product to another organization to use, but our stakeholders were concerned that we would turn into a customer service provider and nixed the idea. We often talked about starting our own company and selling this great product. But we never did. Our team has continued to meet for reunion lunches for 10 years after that successful rollout.

Give your project an end date, because a sudden ending can be a shock to everyone on the team.

Workflow diagrams demonstrate the need for new features. Other ways can include Excel spreadsheets or other diagramming techniques for workflow. Customer need is not enough. You need to do a workflow diagram

The project's mission outcome was to improve the travelers' expense reporting experience by providing automated processing and reimbursement while continuing to record expenses by trip. We successfully achieved the mission outcome, although we continued to add features beyond the time when the stakeholders expected that we would be done.

108

Creating workflow diagrams demonstrated what the user's experience would be if we were to leave out a feature, (e.g., foreign travel). This clarified to the stakeholders that the change was needed. As you add features, these need to be agreed upon by all stakeholders. Figure 17 shows an example of a workflow diagram that helped demonstrate how foreign travelers would need to interact with the system without automation.

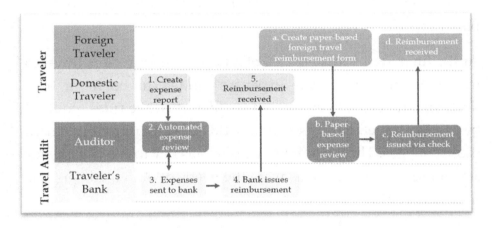

Figure 17. Workflow diagram

Workflow answers the question: Who handles it next? It's a visual representation of a business process that usually utilizes a flowchart. It shows the exact steps needed to complete the process and points out the person who is responsible for each step. Like many other tools, it depicts how the change will impact the user.

In our case, we had a sophisticated process for domestic travelers to get reimbursed electronically through direct deposit. Expense forms are electronically sent to the travel audit team for review and then transmission to the bank where the bank issues reimbursement directly through the traveler's paycheck. Because of unique foreign travel rules (e.g., tax allowance for hotel reimbursement), we were hesitant to add foreign travel to our expense reporting system. Therefore, as shown in the workflow diagram, foreign travelers continued to fill out paper reimbursement forms. Did we really want to continue to process paper forms?

At the time, we estimated 25% of all corporate travelers traveled internationally, and their expenses tended to be more than domestic travelers. Even though we identified the rules required by foreign travel, our stakeholders did not want us to implement those changes. The workflow diagram was key to convincing our stakeholders to proceed, as were the needs of our customers, the travel audit office.

Another major activity in wrapping up a project involves conducting a Lessons Learned activity to help prevent failures from recurrence in future projects. This entire book is based on my Lessons Learned!

Once there is a determination that the project is coming to a close, there are many close-out activities that need to be done, such as re-assigning the staff to another project, finalizing budget numbers, and widely advertising your new operational system. The most important close out activity that sometimes gets overlooked is a Lessons Learned event. Figure 18 shows the steps that are typically conducted during such an event.

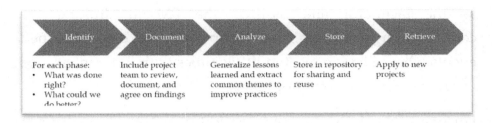

Figure 18. Example Lessons Learned

Conducting a Lessons Learned event should be a repeatable process with a defined formula. In our case, we review what we did right and what could have gone better for each phase of the project. Prior to the meeting, the PM drafts a document, and during the meeting, we walk through each section with all team members giving his or her opinion on the bullet points or contributing other ideas.

In addition, we try to generalize those that could be valuable for future use, documenting them, and storing them in a reusable repository. Stakeholders regularly conduct a review of common themes in order to recommend process changes. For example, if teams tend to complain about the lack of test team availability, then stakeholders can make the appropriate adjustments. In other cases, teams on future projects will often look back on Lessons Learned for similar work to avoid mistakes and mitigate risks.

In my experience with facilitating Lessons Learned activities, team members want to be heard and recognized for what happened. They want closure for things that were both good and bad about the project. I have conducted Lessons Learned events as the facilitator and assisted the PM in drafting the corresponding document. I ran a couple of large Lessons Learned events where I had to meet multiple times with different groups in order to get everyone's opinions.

For one particularly successful project, I presented our lessons learned in a "Project of the Year" award" submission. Those who won year after year could prove to the audience in their lessons learned presentation that they had significantly impacted the business via quantifiable metrics. Whether they saved money or increased the number of responses or benefited in some measurable way, that was the proof they needed. Collect metrics — you'll be glad you did!

As you're getting ready to wrap up a project, or perhaps during another phase, stakeholders may determine that your project needs an independent assessment or a task force review. A task force is an independent group of experts who specifically gather to identify strengths and weaknesses, offer an alternative analysis, or address tactical and execution issues. A task force should identify strengths, weaknesses, opportunities, challenge assumptions, propose alternative strategies, and ultimately lead to improved decision-making and more effective outcomes. If your project has a task force review, you may need to change course, adjust your plans, and focus on outcomes.

I have participated as a technical expert or project manager expert on several task force teams. In each case, I provided a different perspective, creative thinking, and challenged plans in order to reduce risks. Questions I have asked as part of the team have included: Is the opportunity still worth pursuing? Should we proceed as planned or change course? Do we have adequate resources to continue the effort? Do we understand key stakeholders and their issues? Do we need to refine the solution or re-examine the schedule and milestones?

The complexity of today's projects requires leaders to look through multiple lenses. Task force outputs provide the PM with an independent capability to consider concepts, plans, and design from an alternate perspective. In some cases, the ultimate goals and strategy can be aligned by recommending budget allocations and key focus areas in order to shift the organization.

First, you need to pick the members of the task force. Good candidates for team members consist of cross-functional thinkers, subject matter experts in the domain, and those who have experience with similar types of projects. Second, team members receive a description of the effort, the goals for output, and the anticipated time contribution needed. While meeting with the task force, you should give them a sense of ownership and accountability. Target short term solutions to symptoms versus root causes of the issues. Start with the end in mind.

Once the task force completes its assessment, the team members present their recommendations. This can be in the form of a document, white paper, or briefing along with recommended adjustments, such as the schedule, guiding principles, and/or mission outcomes. The recommendations should include areas like key decisions, strategy, and team composition. The task force outputs can provide a gap analysis for the project that the team may incorporate into their plans.

If your project is the subject of a task force, you can buy everyone a T-shirt with a bullseye and get ready to have your project criticized — but also enhanced with new ideas!

Summary

Because a planned completion of a project is better than an abrupt ending, you should plan for the finish line so you can celebrate your successes. That might mean that you need to define the ending before someone else defines it for you. It might also mean you need to argue your case for added functionality using tools such as workflow diagrams. Your project health may need assessment via a task force. Their recommendations may mean modifying plans and goals to tighten and refine the project outcomes. And at the end of the wrap-up activities, shoot for conducting a Lessons Learned activity to give the team an opportunity to speak up as well as to provide you with the opportunity to congratulate them on their successes.

Wrapping up a project can take many forms, such as some last-minute changes or analyses that can improve your outcome. Let's see next what happens in the final stretch of your project as you think about wrapping it up!

CHECKLIST

Controlling - Are We Done Yet?

Are We Done Yet? Move to operational phase, stakeholder review

✓ Be aware of project end-state and be wary when customers want to continually add features

✓ Plan the project ending, know when you are done

✓ Coordinate project end activities, such as rollout and communication plans

✓ Conduct user training, create videos, and consider corporate help desk training

✓ Execute or participate in a task force to conduct a project review, performed by an independent group of experts who address tactical and execution issues, refine solution, and challenge assumptions to improve decision making and have more effective outcomes

Tools and techniques

✓ Develop workflow diagrams when demonstrating whether added functionality is needed and to demonstrate user's experience with or without the new functionality

✓ Use workflow diagrams to answer questions about who handles it next by providing a visual representation of business process via a flowchart

✓ Create other diagrams as needed, including comparison of To-Be vs. As-Is

---

✓ Collect lessons learned for each project phase, what was done right vs. what could have been done better

✓ Generalize lessons learned and extract common themes to change corporate processes

✓ Store in a repository for reuse and apply to future projects as needed

Soft skills: Putting out fires, dedication to the project's success, and not taking business decisions personally.

CHAPTER 9
CLOSING
Wrapping it Up

Model vulnerability and humility, which unsurprisingly helps to create psychological safety in the workplace.

— The Fearless Organization

There was a time when I would buy music CDs. Then the time came when I downloaded music to my mp3 player. And now I use a music streaming service. Each one helped to improve the process of curating my playlist. Just doing things the same way you have done them for years is usually less than optimal. Eventually someone will notice that your process shouldn't take as long as it actually does. And, in some cases, just one little process change can result in a huge savings in time and resources.

Even after projects have been implemented, there is still time for improvement. In the wrap-up phase, you are doing all those things needed to end the project, until questions are raised about finalizing your work. How can it be better, faster, or more beneficial to end users? It may be time to examine your process.

This chapter will discuss how the PM wraps up the project,

including conducting process analysis on any outstanding process delays. Swim lanes can delineate personas and their role in the analysis. Document repositories store exemplar artifacts and prepare for reuse on a similar future project. PMs need to exhibit many characteristics, but resilience is the most important.

Process analysis is a diagramming technique used to evaluate the many steps in completing a task to optimize the process and enhance the user experience. Often these process analysis diagrams depict the current process and point out bottlenecks. They may also divide the tasks into different swim lanes. Even though you're at the finish line, always look for ways to streamline, simplify, and make changes.

Swim lanes are rows or columns used in a diagram to illustrate steps taken by a certain persona or type of user and delineate where hand-offs occur.

Document repositories are used to store significant documentation. Creating such a repository for future reuse means that you include the exemplar documents, such as process analysis diagrams, tag them with meta data, enable search features, and encourage future efforts to reuse them.

Resilience is one of the most important PM characteristics, because projects usually run into challenges. Brainstorming for tools and techniques to resolve these issues will assist with the PM's confidence and resilience needed to push forward and result in a successful outcome. Fail fast, learn, and move on.

Characteristics exhibited during this phase include analytical skills, independence, team working skills, being indispensable and resilience.

You will be surprised how much impact one small change can make to your project in process improvement. This use case illustrates an example of how process analysis made a huge impact.

CASE STUDY

Conduct process analysis to avoid processes taking too long

Remember, if the process is taking too long, time is money. Process analysis can be a powerful tool for saving time. Project optimization can streamline processes and remove unnecessary steps.

To securely connect to corporate systems remotely, all employees are required to use two-factor authentication, including a random number obtained from a physical security token. These tokens had a three-year shelf life, and the process to replace them was taking too long. Analysis of the process showed that we were shipping new deactivated tokens — which forced the recipient to activate them as an additional step. Shipping the token deactivated was a security requirement. We worked with our security engineers to obtain their approval to ship activated tokens, and this cut processing time in half.

In my role as the Business Analyst (BA), I developed process analysis diagrams and recommended ways to avoid time-consuming bottlenecks. I worked closely with the engineer to record his step-by-step approach to token renewals.

The process analysis was complex due to recording the many steps needed to prepare one token to send to an employee, estimating the time required for each step, and identifying any potential opportunities for improvement. The biggest time loss occurred when the employee called to have their token activated. In learning about the product, the vendor expected new tokens to be shipped that were already activated. The vendor even built features into the tokens to protect from theft, including automatically deactivating the old token once the new one was used.

The first step in creating a process analysis was to sit with the administrator and record all required and detailed steps. Once I had that information, I diagrammed it so that the process made sense visually. This involved dividing the process into key steps, for example, preparing the token, mailing it, and then interacting with users. Once these key areas or swim lanes were defined, detailed timelines were added to each section and then assigned an estimated completion time for each item.

As I continued my analysis, my BA techniques guided me, and key issues or critical areas began to pop out from the diagrams. I conducted further vendor research to discover how other clients handle this scenario in order to derive additional recommendations. The solution was to ship the tokens in the activated state to take advantage of the vendor protection features and reduce time to complete by eliminating the need to call for token activation.

In our case, the process analysis had an unplanned side effect of improving the user experience, since they no longer interrupted their day to make that phone call to the administrator for token activation. They just started using the new token. Our stakeholders were happy because the process took less time. Administrators were happy because of fewer interruptions, allowing them to get more work done.

Users were happy because they just started using the new token without any further steps. The vendor was happy because we utilized their already built-in safety features. And our security engineers were happy because we mitigated risks through other means. In this case, optimizing performance minimized resource costs and time, saved money, and made things easier for users.

Our security department has authority over any security-related changes, and they were hesitant to approve this change. After all, they originally required that deactivated tokens be shipped in order to prevent unauthorized access. We presented our risk mitigation factors and security agreed to allow us to ship activated tokens.

The project team needed an unbiased process review, so I provided that guidance and an outside perspective. I applied my experience with process analysis and documented my recommendations in the form of a series of process improvement diagrams, each providing an increasing level of detail. The key action from this work was convincing security to change their rule to ship tokens in a deactivated state. I used my process analysis material to present the risk mitigation factors.

Although this process change may seem small, it had a huge impact on the way people did their jobs. In some cases, the mere act of documenting a complex process can be an eye-opener for seeing bottlenecks that inhibit progress. This was a classic example of demonstrating that work you do as BA and as PM significantly drives the success of a project.

In wrapping up a project, you may need to optimize the process by developing process analysis diagrams. Recommending improvements to streamline the process, and seeing those improvements put in place is a satisfying result. Be sure to advertise the solution via lessons learned and place the results in a reusable repository.

There are many other ways to assess projects aside from process improvement diagrams, including other diagramming techniques like service blueprints, mind maps, journey maps, flow charts, and even spreadsheets.

Use diagramming to highlight process improvements.

The project's mission outcome was to have the whole company of 8,000 employees have their tokens renewed by the expiration date. This was accomplished by shortening the time to renew tokens.

I created Process Analysis diagrams to identify bottlenecks and recommend optimization approaches. Shipping tokens in an activated state was a small change that made a huge impact in accelerating time to impact. Figure 19 shows an example of a process analysis that depicts the various steps taken during token replacement at a high-level.

Figure 19. Process Analysis

Process analysis is the action of conducting a review and gaining an understanding of the business processes in place. It involves reviewing the components of a process and their interactions in order to produce results. New technology can become available, making the as-is processes obsolete. Any diagramming is preceded by a detailed examination and documentation of the current steps. Process analysis diagrams can take many forms, and in our case, we stepped through the user's actions and annotated each step with an estimated time. This example shows the steps from the user's standpoint, which can add a dose of reality to the viewer and put the stakeholders in the user's shoes. Additional versions added more detail including timing calculations.

Stakeholders had an amazingly positive reaction to this effort, given that such a small change would have such a big impact. It has been cited time and again as a great example of the value of process analysis. Here are the steps I took to create this process analysis.

- **Problem definition**: Understand both the process and the vendor product

- **Document**: Sit with users and watch the current process in action

- **Diagramming**: Draw diagrams, giving attention to bottlenecks (a version of a journey map)

- **Re-visit constraints**: In this case, vendor constraints, security, and vendor potential solutions

- **Re-vise diagrams**: Show improvements that can be gained through the suggested process change(s)

Other tools that can be used to improve processes consist of prototyping and storyboarding. In both of these techniques, the project team visually documents use cases and scenarios in order to give a visual picture from the user's perspective. The team can ask questions and scrutinize the plan to encourage optimization.

After we documented this process analysis, we uploaded it as an exemplar to a sharable repository to encourage reuse.

Today's projects use a repository for team and stakeholder sharing. These repositories are used to share documents and store the latest version of critical information in one place. Some common document types that belong on the site include schedules, plans, resource plans, budget plans, requirements documents, user stories, design documents, training plans, change management plans, demo scripts, testing scripts, UAT testing scripts, and key presentations or briefings. As these documents are used throughout the course of the effort, the repository can be used to track changes, keep documents updated, and maintain older copies as needed. Figure 20 shows a sample of the types of documents to include in a reusable repository.

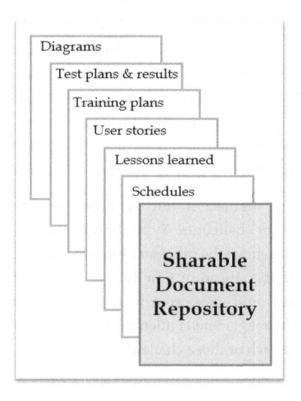

Figure 20. Example of Exemplar Repository Contents

After the project ends, what happens to these documents? If your IT organization is anything like mine, they probably stay in the repository until someone asks for them to be archived. But there are valuable examples of documents in that repository that could likely be used by others. One of the challenges is to connect meta data to these documents so they can be searchable and retrievable. Otherwise, other users will be confused in trying to track down related documents that can be used as templates. A searchable repository is a must, as is a Lessons Learned repository.

We reviewed the document repository within our PM

Community of Practice, which provides like-minded PMs an opportunity to informally discuss challenges, solutions, tools, and guidance. I started such a group in my IT organization, and as long as people continued to bring their challenges to the meetings to discuss alternatives, it continues to be valuable. Other avenues for sharing advice include local PM meetings, conferences, and meetings of IT groups in similar companies.

If you haven't figured it out by now, projects have many opportunities for challenges. Typical problems that occur can be overcome if you have the necessary tools in your arsenal that you can use to predict ahead of time that you are likely to run into these risk areas and then proactively mitigate them. Below are the 8 project management challenges and the case studies herein that illustrate each of those challenges.

TYPICAL PROJECT MANAGEMENT CHALLENGES	ILLUSTRATED IN WHICH CASE STUDY
1. Resources inadequate	1. Limited resources and process too long (Ch. 9)
2. Meeting unrealistic deadlines	2. Scope creep results in extended deadlines (Ch. 4)
3. Unclear goals/direction	3. Minimal guidance (Ch. 3)
4. Team members uncommitted	4. No commitment of budget for HCM RFP (Ch. 2)
5. Insufficient planning	5. Keep adding features for project that never ends (Ch. 8)
6. Breakdown of communications	6. Users unhappy with new scoring technique (Ch. 6)
7. Changes in goals and resources	7. PMO reassigned when changes in resources and budgets (Ch 5)
8. Conflicts between depth of functions	8. Testing errors and rollback effected multiple depts (Ch. 7)
"Project Management — The Managerial Process"	

There are many reasons for project challenges, not only due to the projects themselves, but also because of people issues. For example, when most employees are working remotely, communication effectiveness is generally more difficult, and you must proactively reach out or else there may be disagreements.

The key to getting past project challenges is to just "get over it." Projects do fail on occasion, and you need to be prepared for that eventuality.

And, of course, there are different degrees of challenges, as illustrated by the case studies. Anyone who says there are no challenges on their projects is lying — there are always challenges. Be resilient, get back on your feet, and keep going.

Summary

Process analysis may seem like a small change, yet it can result in huge improvements. Document it so that others gain the knowledge of how to do process improvement themselves. After all, your efforts are critical, relevant, and important to the success of your project.

CHECKLIST
Closing - Wrapping it up

Wrapping it up: Document lessons learned, finalize budget

✓ Advertise your successful operational system internally and externally by publicizing at conferences, social media, other internal avenues

✓ Sell your project to key stakeholders to act as "evangelists," and track usage and other metrics to quantify project impact

---

✓ Consider project issues or challenges as minor setbacks since there are many reasons such as inadequate resources, meeting unrealistic deadlines, unclear goals, and direction

✓ Evaluate whether your documentation could be reused and placed into a reusable repository with connected meta data so that they are searchable and retrievable

✓ Encourage use of valuable examples to jump start the next similar project

Tools and techniques

✓ Address any outstanding questions that may remain even at the last phase of the project, such as how to make project improvements.

✓ Consider conducting a process improvement analysis, since a small change can optimize your process and result in big savings of both time and resources

✓ Create a process analysis diagram to identify gaps and recommend improvements

✓ Conduct a task force review as an individual or as a group to examine how new technology can optimize and improve old processes

✓ Finalize any budget details and reassign project team to new assignments

✓ Wrap up the project with a Lessons Learned analysis, including what was done right, what could have been done better, and how to improve next time

Soft skills: Demonstrate problem solving, analytical skills, independence, team working skills, be indispensable and resilient

CHAPTER 10
CONCLUSION

There is no other choice. When we look closely, we recognize the same balls being dropped over and over, even by those of great ability and determination. We know the patterns. We see the costs. It's time to try something else. Try a checklist.

—Atul Gawande

Be honest — most projects run into challenges, and your job is to avoid problems, delays, and cost overruns. PMs often rely on an arsenal of tools to prevent, solve, and resolve challenges. Had we been more honest with ourselves prior to kick off, we might have predicted that there would be no budget, that the rollout would fail, that the project might never end, or that the users would not like it. Applying these techniques can support your team to focus on execution and deliver successful outcomes.

The BA and PM can combine forces to be more successful in project endeavors, and the ideal scenario is when you have the budget for one of each on your project. Otherwise, combining these two skill sets can drive mission success. The problem with PMs who have no BA skills is that they are looked upon as task managers — people who can only do Kanban boards, but who don't understand all the requirements or process flows. If you just have a BA or systems engineer and no PM, your team may lack organization, delegation, scheduling, and stakeholder communication skills. The skills of both the BA and PM are critical, depending on requests and what is needed, to drive project success. They are the linchpin to project complexity, managing remote teams, creating new business, and being a recognized leader.

In recommending approaches for each phase of a project, the case studies I have presented are real life examples of my projects. In all cases, there was an issue that needed to be solved. Presenting a set of game-changer tools for each phase provides a step-by-step approach for you at each stage. These actionable and tangible tools can only be learned by trying them out on your own project.

In addition, the summary checklists at the end of each chapter should be reminders of typical challenges that you should watch out for and what you need to do to address them. I am a huge fan of checklists, and I use them all the time. Your project's success will be directly proportional to the amount of planning and advance thinking you have done.

By applying the guidance and ideas I've presented in this book, you can develop a "get-well" plan for your project and take action right now to set things right. Why do you need a get-well plan? Perhaps you don't have the luxury of an independent task force assessment but feel the need to conduct your own internal review in order to make improvements. What are the steps and how do you go about executing such a get-well plan?

First review phase (2-4 weeks, depending on project size): Start out in the first phase by ensuring you have the As-Is documentation for your project. These can be in any format, including documents, slides, and/or spreadsheets. These materials can provide insight into your project and where things may have gone wrong or need fixing.

- What was the expected schedule and where are you now?
- What was the original problem description?
- Were there any alternatives examined?
- Where was the Work Breakdown Structure?
- What were the most recent status reports?
- Were there any UAT test plan results?

In addition, the team can demonstrate how they have incorporated leadership, team building, and managed diverse groups and/or ideas during this period. Once these collections of items are reviewed, the task force can determine how to proceed and define their recommendations.

Second review phase (2-4 weeks): Once the materials are received and reviewed by the task force, recommendations can be made. Examples of these recommendations include the following possibilities:

- Adjust process diagrams
- Change workflow diagrams

- Modify Kanban boards

- Make changes to persona descriptions

- Conduct a pre-mortem (if this hasn't been done already)

- Conduct a change-readiness review

In addition, the team can demonstrate how they are successfully utilizing the PMO and conducting the test program or task force review. The team can decide whether to proceed with the recommendations, depending on many factors, like whether there is time in the schedule for wholesale changes, available resources, and an appetite for proceeding as described.

Last review phase (2-4 weeks): Finally, the task force can work with the overall team to assist with the move to an operational environment. These final items may include:

- Developing an organizational change management plan

- Collecting success measures and metrics for proof of success

- Conducting lessons learned to allow the team to discuss the pros and cons of the project

- Moving significant documentation to a repository

In addition, resource monitoring will move staff from one project to another as projects end and new ones begin. The team will demonstrate project manager resilience as they experience issues and recover from working on the project.

PROJECT GET-WELL PLAN		
FIRST REVIEW PHASE	**SECOND REVIEW PHASE**	**LAST REVIEW PHASE**
Review As-Is products Schedules Problem definition Alternatives via journey maps Work Breakdown Structure Status Reports UAT Test Plan results	**Adjust follow-on products** Process diagrams Workflow diagrams Kanban boards Personas Risks via Premortem Change Readiness Review	**Prepare move to operational environment** Change Management Success Measures Lessons Learned Project Repository
Soft skills Demonstrate Leadership Build Team Build Agile/Diverse Teams	**Soft skills** Successful use of PMO Conduct Test Plan Conduct task force review	**Soft skills** Conduct Resource Mgt Project Manager Resilience
Review docs, get-well plan	**Adjust project plans**	**Wrap up project**

The above table provides a good way to summarize the material through the various case studies and game-changer tools. You can use this material to guide your get-well plan or use the items individually as you work through your various stages. Prepare for challenges and collect tools to resolve challenges and move forward.

Alas, we do not always have the foresight or the honesty to persevere in being ready for challenges. So instead, we prepare ourselves with an arsenal of tools to dig us out of these challenges. Of the many techniques, figure 21 shows the tools that I use on every project and I consider the most critical for the PM to ensure successful delivery on schedule, budget and performance. These are my recommended game-changer tools to maximize the project success in these areas.

Most Important	PM Tools	BA Tools
Schedule	Schedule	Work breakdown structure
Cost	Budget	Scope management
Performance	Stakeholder Communications	Journey Maps & similar diagramming tools

Figure 21. _Critical PM and BA Techniques_

You can see from the use cases how impactful the positive results can be. Learn how to execute these tools and techniques, and then use them on all of your future projects.

There is no question that being a PM is a challenging role! Are you up for the challenge?

ACKNOWLEDGMENTS

I owe a tremendous debt of gratitude to the many people who have helped make *The Successful Project Manager* a reality. First and foremost are my many colleagues who have tested these ideas, challenged them, refined them, and improved them. Without their relentless and irreplaceable work every day, none of this would be possible. Thank you.

Real projects involve challenges, embarrassing mistakes and oftentimes chaos. I have been grateful throughout my career to have mentors and collaborators who have pushed me to accomplish more than I could have on my own. Thanks to Chad Searfoss who has trusted me with the opportunity to try out many of these ideas. He also had an enormous influence over the shape of this book through his suggestions and recommended changes. His candor and clarification on many of the stories herein improved the book's message, viewpoint and thesis. He witnessed most of it first-hand, so his insights were invaluable.

It takes a community to build a successful project. So many have stepped forward over the years to answer the hard questions, helped me to create projects that were bigger than any one individual, and achieve mission outcomes that seemed impossible at the time. Thanks to my many colleagues whose contributions and dedication were second to none, and they made our project success a team effort. Thank you to: Thom Brando, Michal Cenkl, Christine Cho, Donna Cuomo, Dana

Dornbusch, Charlotte Farmer, Joel Jacobs, Susan Kamener, Dean Kendall, Bob Lesch, Bill Mack, Tom Maher, Deb Mastronardi, Annette Moore, Rob Perfetti, Dan Poltar, Jimmy Providakes, Jon Raymond, John Robidoux, Chad Searfoss, Sal Sganga, Hale Sheikerz, Dan Sorensen, Mike Stradling, Mike Tice, Lynda Thimble, Julie Trudeau, and John Wilson.

Thanks to the hundreds of students at 3 universities (Northeastern University, Boston University, and Babson College) who have given me inspiration and strength by exploring the terrain of technology and project management with open eyes. Thank you to: Joe Griffin, Michael Jocelyn, Meredith Sittmann, Mahaboob Shaik, and too many other students to name.

Those who have had the misfortune of reading an early draft know just how much gratitude I owe to Dave James, who provided essential editorial help. If you enjoyed any part of this book, he deserves your thanks. Also, I want to give a shout out to my reviewers who were brave enough to have their testimonial printed on the cover: Joel Jacobs, Derek Langone, Jeff Rubin, Lou Shipley, and Dan Ward.

I am very grateful to my family who helped me so much. Special thanks to my daughter Rachel, who designed the cover and back cover with style, expertise, and technique. She is the greatest cover designer ever. She also helped with editing, and her suggestions added structure and clarity. My daughters Jennifer and Amanda and my mother Gloria provided the encouragement, support, and enthusiasm I needed to get me across the finish line. Special thanks to my awesome husband, Stephen. From reading early drafts to giving advice on format, to being my biggest cheerleader, he was as important to this book getting done as I was. Always and forever.

REFERENCES

Lawson, C., Lawson, E. (2020). *Project Management — The Managerial Process 8th Edition*. McGraw-Hill Education.

Project Management Institute (2017). *A Guide to the Project Management Body of Knowledge (PMBOK Guide)-Sixth Edition*. Project Management Institute.

International Institute of Business Analysts (2015). *A Guide to the Business Analysis Body of Knowledge (BABOK Guide)*. International Institute of Business Analysis.

Gawande, A (2011). *The Checklist Manifesto*. Picador.

Sandberg, S (2013). *Lean In*. Knopf.

Kim, G, Behr, K., Spafford, G. (2018). *The Phoenix Project*. IT Revolution Press.

Egolt, D. (2001). *Forming, Storming, Norming, Performing*. iUniverse.

Sinek, S. (2017). *Leaders Eat Last: Why Some Teams Pull Together and Others Don't*. Portfolio.

Gates, M (2019). *The Moment of Lift*. Flatiron Books.

Brown, B. (2015), *Daring Greatly*. Avery.

Green, C., Howe, A. (2012). *The Trusted Advisor Field Book: A Comprehensive Toolkit for Leading with Trust*. John Wiley & Sons.

Edmonson, A. (2019), *The Fearless Organization: Creating Psychological Safety in the Workplace for Learning, Innovation, and Growth.* Harvard Business School, John Wiley & Sons.

Innovation Toolkit at: http://itk.mitre.org

AUTHOR'S BIOGRAPHY

Donna Gregorio is an author, seasoned Project Manager, Business Analyst, and Department Head in the IT division of a large strategic consulting company. She is the writer of numerous publications on Project Management, and this is her first book. Donna is the recipient of 17 awards, including Project of the Year and sits on the presentation review committee for IEEE conferences. She has lectured in Project Management Principles at Northeastern University and other prestigious Boston-area colleges. Donna established her company's Project Manager Community of Practice and began her career as a software developer for mission-critical systems, many of which are still in use today. She earned certifications in PMP, CBAP, PMP-Agile, ITIL and Agile Scrum Master/Product Owner. She holds a BS in Computer Science and Mathematics from Tufts University and an MS in Computer Engineering from Northeastern University.

Feel free to connect and continue the conversation at
www.linkedin.com/donna-gregorio
or
www.DonnaGregorio.com.